Law and Democracy in the New Russia

D1739055

Brookings Dialogues on Public Policy

The presentations and discussions at Brookings conferences and seminars often deserve wide circulation as contributions to public understanding of issues of national importance. The Brookings Dialogues on Public Policy series is intended to make such papers and commentary available to a broad and general audience. The series supplements the Institution's research publications by reflecting the contrasting, often lively, and sometimes conflicting views of elected and appointed government officials, other leaders in public and private life, and scholars. In keeping with their origin and purpose, the Dialogues are not subjected to the same formal review procedures established for the Institution's research publications. Brookings publishes the contributions to the Dialogues in the belief that they are worthy of public consideration but does not assume responsibility for their objectivity and for the accuracy of every factual statement. And, as in all Brookings publications, the judgments, conclusions, and recommendations presented in the Dialogues should not be ascribed to the trustees, officers, or other staff members of the Brookings Institution.

Law and Democracy in the New Russia

Edited by

BRUCE L. R. SMITH

GENNADY M. DANILENKO

THE BROOKINGS INSTITUTION / Washington, D.C.

To the memory of

Ed A. Hewett

Editors' Preface

This volume grew out of a January 1993 conference held in Washington, D.C., and jointly sponsored by Brookings and the Gruter Institute for Law and Behavioral Research. The conference brought together American, western European, and Russian legal scholars and jurists to discuss recent constitutional and legal developments in the Russian Federation. The Gruter Institute had previously assembled a small team of American and western European scholars to visit Moscow for preliminary conversations with Russian officials and scholars. A number of the persons visited subsequently attended the January conference.

We conceived of this conference as truly a joint effort to think through the problems of constitutionalism facing the new Russia, and not as an instance of Americans and western Europeans prescribing remedies for the problems faced by Russians. It was also our conviction that a mix of practitioners and scholars would be a fruitful combination to stimulate the debate and dialogue. Our hopes were amply fulfilled in this regard. The discussion was at a high level and enriched the understanding of the participants. The published papers reflect in some cases substantial revisions made by the authors in light of the conference discussions.

Financial support from the Gruter Institute helped make the conference possible. We owe a special measure of gratitude to the Gruter Institute's president and founder, Dr. Margaret Gruter. She has brought a new perspective to the study of legal affairs through her own scholarly writings and has shown a unique capacity to stimulate and motivate others. Dr. Gruter's vision and pioneering spirit were the driving forces behind the conference, and we happily acknowledge our indebtedness to her.

We also wish to thank all our colleagues who collaborated with us in this effort. Our coauthors were a pleasure to work with throughout the project and were patiently supportive as we readied the manuscript for publication. Clifford Gaddy and Bruce MacLaury made helpful comments on drafts of some of the chapters. Caroline Lalire and James Schneider provided valuable editorial assistance. Blake S. Jones verified sources and served as research assistant. Majorie Crow typed numerous drafts under a tight deadline, and Susan Woollen prepared the manuscript for typesetting. Lee Ann Sonnergren and Susan Williams ably assisted in the conference arrangements. Maxim Sidorov handled the interpretation duties for the conference with great skill and also was a valued colleague in planning and arranging the Gruter Institute's initial visit to Moscow.

Russia is undergoing a historic process of transformation. Although beset with difficulties, the process is remarkable for both the pace and scope of change. We hope that this volume casts some useful light on the complex processes of change that are under way, and also contributes to the practical realization of the rule of law in Russia.

The views expressed in this volume are those of the authors and participants and should not be ascribed to the Gruter Institute or to Brookings, or to their trustees, officers, or other staff members.

Contents

Contributors

Robert D. Cooter is professor of law and economics at the Boalt Hall School of Law, University of California at Berkeley.

Gennady M. Danilenko is the head of the Center for International Law at the Institute of State and Law, Russian Academy of Sciences, Moscow.

E. Donald Elliott is Julien and Virginia Cornell Professor of Environmental Law and Litigation at Yale Law School, and a former general counsel at the Environmental Protection Agency.

Wolfgang Fikentscher is professor of law at the University of Munich Law School and also a member of the Max-Planck-Institute for Foreign and International Patent, Copyright, and Competition Law.

Gordon P. Getty is a consultant, musician, and independent scholar from San Francisco.

Robert E. Litan was a senior fellow in the Brookings Economic Studies program at the time of the conference, and is now deputy assistant attorney general–designate in the Antitrust Division of the U.S. Department of Justice.

Bruce L. R. Smith is a member of the senior staff in the Center for Public Policy Education at Brookings.

Vasily A. Vlasihin is the head of U.S. legal studies at the Institute of the USA and Canada, Russian Academy of Sciences, Moscow.

BRUCE L. R. SMITH

Constitutionalism in the New Russia

Democracy, by most definitions, involves three elements: pluralism (the distribution of power among government units and between government and society); competing political groups or individuals (who seek office in regularly scheduled and honest elections); and secure civil liberties (protection by law of the rights of free speech, freedom from arbitrary arrest, free exercise of the ballot, and so forth). Some definitions, such as those of Joseph Schumpeter and Samuel Huntington, stress *process* rights—the competition for power and the electoral process—and leave aside results, outcomes, the social safety net, and rights other than those required by the open and fair competition for power.[1]

Stressing process rights, Freedom House, in its annual survey, divides nations into three categories: free, partly free, and not free. By its metric, the past few decades have seen "the greatest expansion of freedom in history. Over one-third of the nations on earth, encompassing nearly 30 percent of the earth's population, have consciously decided to radically alter their political systems for more open and democratic forms of government." Last year's survey "recorded the freest year in its 21-year history. It was the first year in which both the number of Free countries and their populations outnumbered the Not Free countries and their populations. . . . The number of Free societies continued to rise to an all-time high of 76. More remarkably still, the *Survey* found that there were 91 democracies and another 35 countries in some form of democratic transition—a staggering 126 out of the 183 nations evaluated—compared to 44 democracies in 1972 and 56 in 1980."[2]

Russia has moved into the category of partly free, along with the Baltic states and the nations of eastern and central Europe. But what, in practice, does this mean? How far has Russia developed toward becoming a stable democracy? What remains to be done to ensure continued progress? Addressing these questions satisfactorily is a daunting challenge. There is, however, scarcely a more important topic. If the former Soviet Union becomes a stable democracy, the example will inevitably influence the political development of the other nations that were once a part of the Soviet empire. And the prospects for a peaceful and prosperous world will be immeasurably enhanced.

One must confront at the outset the need to distinguish the appearance of democratic institutions from the reality of constitutional governance. From the earliest times, of course, some communities endeavored to govern according to written law. The ancient empires of the Near East, the Greek city-states, and Rome followed their own versions of constitutionalism.[3] Even the former Soviet Union had a constitution that was impressive in the liberties accorded—on paper at least—to citizens. Starting in the late 1950s, Moscow made efforts to codify Soviet law. This first reform impulse led to the adoption of the Soviet constitution in 1977.[4] Legislative reforms associated with the constitution resulted in additional measures to systematize and modernize the law, notable among them the publication in 1980, for the first time, of a multivolume collection of Soviet laws.[5] But despite periodic attempts to update an "open" body of laws, there remained a significant body intended for internal bureaucratic use only.[6] The basic relationship of the citizen to the state and the substantive function of law as an instrument of state power did not change significantly during these initial phases of legal reform.

A more important but still circumscribed reform phase began early in Mikhail Gorbachev's presidency. The need for reform, including reform of the legal system, was widely recognized, and the atmosphere had improved for public discussion. But the efforts at legal reform, like much of Gorbachev's program in other areas, fell short of significant change. The high point of this phase was reached in August 1986, when the Council of Ministers and the president of the Supreme Soviet adopted a plan setting forth a timetable for the enactment of thirty-eight legislative acts reforming various aspects of the economy, government activities, and the legal institutes.[7] Few of the measures were actually enacted, however, because the agenda was overtaken by broader and more sweeping reform proposals as *glasnost* and *perestroika* gathered momentum.

Legal reform received real impetus in 1987 with the reemergence of the concept of the "rule-of-law" state or "law-governed state" (*pravovoye gosudarstvo*). This concept, which had been called bourgeois by authorities and been denied any place in Soviet law or institutions, became the point around which legal *perestroika* and increasingly other reform efforts were organized. The concept was close to the German *Rechtsstaat*, incorporating the ideas of written (and openly published) law, transparency and regularity of procedure, and conformance to law in official behavior. But the *Rechtsstaat* in modern democratic theory has become broadened to embody such wider concepts as citizen participation in government, protection of human rights, separation of powers, and (at least in American thinking) the validity of higher law and popular sovereignty. American ideals have become particularly impotent in Russia, especially Madisonian ideas of limited government and the balance of powers as ways to protect individual liberty. The law-governed state is clearly a concept important for Russia and the other nations of the former Soviet empire, but the challenge remains to delineate its full practical implications and to distinguish the meaning of law in a democratic state from its meaning in a communist state.

The practical issues as well as the philosophical questions now facing Russia were the subject of a conference sponsored by the Brookings Institution and the Gruter Institute in January 1993. The conference drew together constitutional scholars and justices from Russia, other European countries, and the United States. In this introductory chapter I present the issues discussed at the conference as well as my own views on matters relating to democracy in Russia.

CURRENT STATUS OF THE RULE OF LAW AND DEMOCRACY IN RUSSIA

One must be impressed, as a point of departure, with the remarkable progress that has been achieved since the advent of *perestroika* in June 1987. Civil liberties are now well respected in Russia. Freedom of expression, free exercise of religion, and the absence of arbitrary arrest seem to have been largely ensured. Since the collapse of the August 1991 coup against Mikhail Gorbachev, political rights, such as the right to organize and compete for power, have also flourished. Elections have been held (under varying rules and with some notable differences) for the presidency of Russia, the Congress of People's Deputies, and the Supreme Soviet. The important referendum on President Boris Yeltsin's leadership and economic reforms held in April 1993 was the most recent expression of popular participation in the governing process. A constitutional structure embodying elements of the separation of powers has been set in place. Discussions have continued, apparently at an accelerating pace, on a new constitution. In short, the institutional features that constitute democratic government are beginning to be present in more than embryo, if less than fully developed, form.

The visitor to Russia cannot help but be impressed by what has been accomplished. Contact with public officials at federal, regional, and local levels leaves one with a deep admiration for the new Russia. Problems of great magnitude have been faced. The will to achieve a "normal" (that is, Western and free) society is manifest. However, the movement toward democracy, the rule of law and respect for human rights, so notable in the Russian Federation itself, has progressed much less or only minimally in certain other republics.

What is lacking in Russia? Perhaps the most serious problem with the current state of democracy is the underdevelopment of the political parties and the political immaturity of many new politicians. There is an absence of what has been called "civic culture."[8] The forms and institutions of democracy are developing, but the spirit is missing. This lack of civility makes political compromise and day-to-day cooperation difficult. The inflammatory political rhetoric makes even rough-and-ready American politics seem tame.

Changes need to be made in legal practice and political institutions, but they are potentially less significant than developing the attitudes and values that would build the spirit of a working democracy. At the start of the conference Wolfgang Fikentscher noted that countries have fundamental values and traditional styles that often surface in times of crisis and provide guides for action. Pointing to the presbytery in America, the common law tradition in Britain, and the *verein* (association) in Germany, he asked, what ultimate set of values guides Russia now that communist ideology is discredited? Is Russia now a state without an ideology? The Russian and American participants debated whether such deep-rooted values might be found partly in the prerevolutionary tensions between nationalism and Westernism, as embodied, for example, in the contrasts between Fyodor Dostoyevski and Ivan Turgenev. The concept of *pravovoye gosudarstvo* itself first appeared in the Czarist era. The rule of law and democracy are universal concepts that have deep appeal to Russians, but they must be rooted in particular cultural values if they are to grow and flourish.

Fikentscher stimulated discussion on the sequence of steps required to establish a rule-of-law state and a free market economy. Patterned

on the German *Wirtschaftswunder* (economic miracle) after World War
✓ II, reform of labor laws to encourage savings would be the critical first
step. Measures to ensure law and order would follow closely, then
✓ measures to enforce competition. Only in the final stages would de-
control of prices occur. Fikentscher inquired whether the Russian experience had reversed this sequence, whether price liberalization had
proceeded too rapidly before the legal framework was firmly in place.
He drew attention to the paucity of useful thinking in Western economic literature about transforming a command economy into a market economy and considered the linkage between law and economic
behavior a fertile ground for further research. Other participants challenged the idea that locking the Russian Federation into a European-
style labor rights regime should be the first priority. This approach,
they contended, could block the development of a genuine market
economy.

Differences of opinion about the virtues of German-style *soziale
Marktwirtschaft* (social market economy) as opposed to the more free-
wheeling American pluralist market economy recurred often in the conference. The Russian participants, trying to avoid offending either the
Europeans or their American hosts, found merit in both approaches.
They were, indeed, eager to compromise by appearing to embrace American political institutions and German economic institutions. All participants agreed that progress had been made in Russia: the Yeltsin government had at least embarked on a reform course, a sharp contrast to the
dithering that occurred late in the *perestroika* period.

THE COMMITMENT TO A NEW
WRITTEN CONSTITUTION

Does Russia need a new written constitution or can it merely amend
the old one? This question needs further examination. If possible, the
issue should be set apart from the immediate political problems that
have produced the gridlock in Russian politics—the paralyzing dispute on the respective powers of the executive and the legislature. Of
course, one cannot entirely separate the larger issue from the tangle
of related short-term political problems any more than America's
Founding Fathers could when the U.S. Constitution was adopted.
✓ Russia is seeking a new constitutional order just as the Founding
Fathers sought to fix the faults of the regime established by the Articles

of Confederation. The Founding Fathers confronted whether they must be bound by the decision rules laid down by the Articles of Confederation or whether they could redefine their instructions, write a new constitution (rather than amend the old one), and invent new requirements (less than unanimous approval, for example) for ratification. Russia too must realize a new constitutional order without destroying the idea of constitutionalism.

The West, and the United States in particular, may have misled Russia by stressing too much the importance of a written constitution. Hungary has achieved a great deal of freedom and a working democratic system without adopting a new constitution. Similarly, Poland has achieved rapid progress with an odd combination of old communist structures and emerging democratic institutions. Their experience suggests that democratic behavior can coexist and even prosper within a seemingly archaic framework. The new order can gradually transform the old.

Yet the current awkward political structure in Russia—both the Supreme Soviet and the Congress of People's Deputies claim power, and there are other institutional anomalies—apparently cannot be remedied without a changed constitution. Some Russian colleagues also believe that civil liberties cannot be adequately safeguarded without a formal bill of rights adopted with a new constitution, even though substantial protection of civil rights has been achieved by amendments to the 1977 Constitution. However, weak protection of rights in a new constitution might create conditions worse than the present situation. According to Gennady Danilenko in this volume, 75 percent of the 1977 Constitution has already been amended and a great many protections of civil and human rights have been incorporated. Indeed, the Russian Constitution has incorporated many of the human rights guaranteed under the Helsinki Treaty and other instruments of international law.

The constitutional amendments and legal changes that have already occurred, one might argue, represent a sufficient basis for a law-governed state. Adoption of a new written constitution might thus add little beyond what has been achieved. A new constitution will have been created anyway as further incremental changes occur through action by the legislature and the courts. This approach reflects the idea that constitutionalism means the totality of the laws, customs, and procedures whereby a nation governs itself. This usage might be loosely characterized as a "living constitution"—an English conception—in contrast to the more American idea of a constitution antecedent to and setting the ground rules for normal politics. There is no doubt that Russia's struggles through daily crises have begun to define a kind of constitutionalism. But most Russians evidently prefer the idea of a constitution that is more fundamental than everyday political struggles. This still leaves room for debate, however, on the relative merits of British and American conceptions of jurisprudence. Although in Britain any current government must answer to the higher law of tradition and to the spirit of British institutions as embodied in such documents as the Magna Carta and the Bill of Rights of 1689, Parliament remains the sovereign expositor of the law of the land. In America, a tradition of appeal to a higher or natural law prevails as the yardstick by which to judge what is lawful authority, and the Supreme Court, not the legislature, is entrusted with the ultimate responsibility.[9]

The postreferendum situation in Russia clearly calls for an effort to resolve at least the most critical issues by at least adopting a new constitution and then holding new parliamentary elections. Although it seems likely that Russia will now at last complete the process of drafting and ratifying a new constitution, how this will occur and which versions of three separate drafts will actually be adopted remain unclear. The most recent draft was advanced by President Yeltsin in the aftermath of his success in the April 1993 referendum and contained provisions for a much stronger executive than existed in previous draft constitutions debated by the legislature.

The issues that remain to be resolved are numerous and complex. Should the constitution be long, attempting to resolve many outstanding issues, or short, merely sketching the framework for the new system and leaving to the future the resolution of the major issues? Where should the basic division of powers be between executive and legislative branches? Should regional or local officials, or both, be appointed or directly elected? What authority should be retained at the federal level and what devolved to regional units (bearing in mind that the Russian Federation itself could dissolve into a welter of new sovereignties)? Finally, how should whatever new constitution is proposed be ratified?

In 1989 the new Congress of Peoples' Deputies created the Committee on Constitutional Supervision under the chairmanship of academician S. A. Aleekseyev to oversee the drafting of a new document. Subsequently a committee within the Supreme Soviet took over the task. The new constitution was scheduled to be presented to the Supreme Soviet in late November 1992, and its members were to have two or three months to discuss the draft. This timetable was derailed toward the end of 1992 when the draft was caught up in the escalating dispute between President Yeltsin and his former allies in the congress. There is no easy way to describe the lines of political fracture between Yeltsin and, in particular, the chairman of the Supreme Soviet, Ruslan L. Khasbulatov, but several aspects of the struggle relating to constitutional issues may be noted. The post of chairman of the Supreme Soviet is an oddity, seeming to confer executive powers and inviting efforts to confine the president to a merely ceremonial role. The two legislative chambers, the Congress of Peoples' Deputies and the Supreme Soviet, sometimes work at cross purposes. The whole system, which has both an independent president (American-style or perhaps French-style) and a vote-of-no-confidence provision (British parliamentary-style), seems an incongruous arrangement that cannot function well over the long run.

The confusion at present about the meaning of *law* is in some ways reminiscent of difficulties during the communist era, when the Politboro, the Council of Ministers, the Supreme Soviet, and various ministers and enterprises all claimed to be issuing binding laws. The laws were not fully published or adequately disseminated, and conflicts about the priority among laws inevitably resulted. The Congress of Peoples' Deputies initially conferred upon President Yeltsin the power to issue decrees having the force of law, but in December 1992 this power lapsed and was not renewed. The congress henceforth asserted that *it* was the government and that the president had no authority to take any action without prior congressional authorization. The president alternately sought compromise and escalated his attacks on the congress. The dispute came to a head in March 1993 when, in an address to the nation, Yeltsin indicated that he might be forced to invoke emergency powers. In the furious maneuvering that followed the speech, the Constitutional Court, under Chairman Valery Zorkin, emerged in an influential, if sometimes more political than judicial, role.

The referendum held in April 1992 provided an impressive vote of confidence for the Yeltsin government. As a result, elections for the parliament appeared likely to occur before the scheduled 1995 date. But the most critical item on the public agenda was the fate of the constitution, for only constitutional change could define the nature of the parliament to be elected and accelerate the parliamentary elections.

The extent of executive and legislative powers was a key constitutional issue at the January 1993 conference and occasioned a lively debate. According to some Russian participants, the gridlock between the president and the Supreme Soviet has not been wholly unhealthy. Executive-legislative tension, even though resulting in inaction at times, has meant that President Yeltsin is forced to accept the Supreme Soviet as a legitimate body; he cannot simply sidestep the legislature and govern by decree.

Conference participants from Russia, other European countries, and the United States agreed that authority must derive from the legislature in a rule-of-law state, but the perspectives of European and American participants toward inherent or residual executive authority differed. In America the state governments are the governments of general jurisdiction and have so-called police powers (the ability to act on behalf of the health, welfare, and safety of citizens) that are the functional equivalent of the residual executive authority of the French president or the British Crown as exercised by the cabinet. The American federal executive has no residual or inherent authority, and the federal government as a whole can exercise only limited and enumerated powers.

President Yeltsin's position has elements of Charles de Gaulle's situation when he moved from the Fourth to the Fifth Republic in 1958 and is also somewhat analogous to that of the American colonists who sought to transcend the Articles of Confederation. After the April 1993 referendum, Yeltsin summoned a special assembly of regional leaders at which he presented a new draft for a constitution that, evidently drawing heavily on the work of academician Aleekseyev who had earlier headed the Committee on Constitutional Supervision, differed sharply from two drafts under consideration in the legislature. Yeltsin's draft enlarged the powers of the presidency along the lines of those wielded by the French president and limited the role of the legislature. Apparently convinced that the Congress of Peoples' Deputies would never accept his constitutional views, Yeltsin has decided to circumvent the legislature and achieve ratification through either a special constitutional convention or a referendum, or some combination of the two. As of summer 1993 a working draft incorporating features of the three constitutional drafts remains to be achieved. Yeltsin's dilemma seems to be that in turning to the regional leaders to preserve his presidential prerogatives vis-à-vis the legislature, he could be forced to trade away to the regions too many powers of the central government.

AMERICAN SEPARATION OF POWERS AND EUROPEAN PARLIAMENTARIANISM

Because Russians have evidently expressed a preference for a separation-of-powers rather than a Westminster model of democracy, a brief discussion of the separation-of-powers system is in order. The American system, much admired by Russians, is actually one in which separate institutions share powers. The best interaction between the executive power and the legislative is not decided once and for all by any formula. Instead, working relationships evolve gradually. Tensions among the powers are natural and will always be present. But according to many conference participants, a few practical changes could improve working relations. In practice, some blend of American separation of powers with European parliamentarianism seems to be evolving.

Confirmation of Executive Officials

The prime minister and perhaps four or five key cabinet ministers should be confirmed by the parliament. Prime ministers in general should have political links to the parliament even if they are not members so as to help build a working coalition between the two branches (or, at least, the highest executive officials should be politicians rather than bureaucrats). Tension between technocratic and political perspectives was clearly a problem with the prime ministership of Yigor Gaider. Although a brilliant economist and administrator, the former prime minister lacked ties to any parliamentary faction. Initially President Yeltsin considered this a great asset, but the absence of political linkages made it more difficult to forge effective working relationships between the executive and legislative branches.

Part of the problem was ambiguity over the proper role of the new Russian prime minister. Did the office, in fact, constitute an awkward imposition of Westminster elements upon a separation-of-powers system? A first step in answering is to think through whether one wants to develop a political system that includes elements of a British-style parliamentary model, stay squarely with the U.S. separation-of-powers model, or embrace a mixed form. A mixed system seems the preferred choice—or so many Russian participants said. Under any conception the legislature should have some real powers. Legislative confirmation of the executive's high-level appointments is one obvious step toward the genuine sharing of power. But the roles and responsibilities of executive and legislature are at present undeniably confused in Russia. The legislature tries to run everything and ends up running nothing. The executive branch does not always seem clear whether it is acting in accord with law, creating law, actually initiating a program, or merely declaring policy goals. In light of the referendum's results, however, these relationships will most likely become clarified. Already, as the new political parties have gained experience in the arts of democratic governance, more realistic expectations have emerged and extreme positions have been moderated.

The Budget Process

Russia needs an orderly budget process, at a minimum something similar to the system set up under the U.S. Budget and Accounting Act of 1921. But making the process work encompasses two processes: effective executive writing of the budget and effective legislative review of the budget. The Supreme Soviet or successor parliament cannot develop a budget de novo. The executive must first submit a budget with some coherence. This will require, among other things, a Treasury or an Office of Management and Budget to assist the prime minister, a greater degree of integration within the executive branch (that is, control over ministries and subministries), and a career civil service to work with the appointed officials closest to the president and prime minister.

The president's office was reorganized in the spring of 1993, and an experienced legislator, Sergey A. Filatov, formerly first deputy chairman of the Supreme Soviet, was installed as chief of staff to assist President Yeltsin. Obviously, complex policy issues were at stake here that outweighed management principles. But as all participants at the January conference agreed, the new democratic government before this move had failed to function effectively on a day-to-day practical level. Russia needed to achieve a more orderly decisionmaking system and to be less driven by crisis-induced improvisation. A well-run administrative apparatus was required, and Filatov helped achieve that purpose.

Executive Discretion

The amount of authority vested in the executive, and the extent to which it is regulated by legislative and judicial action, is critical to the concept of a law-governed state. Limited power to issue decrees was conferred on the president in 1991 by the Congress of People's Deputies. But although Yeltsin and his aides believed he exercised restraint in using that power, Congress did not think so and stripped him of it in late 1992.

The problem in broad outline might be phrased thus: a modus operandi must be devised that allows the legislature to set bounds to the exercise of power but still empowers the executive to act. One solution is for the legislature to reserve for itself a form of legislative veto. Oversight by the legislature or a major committee would provide a better means of controlling administrative action than attempting to bind the executive too closely by detailed laws. The executive-legislative gridlock of 1992–93 was created by disputes over which branch would have the right to appoint and remove key officers of the government, which would have final budgetary power (especially over the budgets of the state-run enterprises) and which would control the money supply (under the current system the Central Bank has been under the control of the congress). Other disputes included how extensive executive discretion would be (some elements of the congress insisted that the president had no powers, only ceremonial duties) and who would control the state television stations.

By the spring of 1993 there was virtually no common ground left that would permit orderly governing. Several times a compromise appeared at hand between Yeltsin and his chief parliamentary rival (and former close ally) Ruslan L. Khasbulatov, only to fall apart and provoke a deeper rift. The referendum on April 28, 1993, produced a stunning 58 percent approval vote for Yeltsin and a 53 percent majority approving his reform policies. Results for the referendum questions on early congressional and presidential elections were less conclusive.[10]

STRENGTHENING THE JUDICIAL SYSTEM

As the new democratic order in Russia struggles to be born, general concern with the rule of law has increasingly focused on the role of the judiciary. In a compressed period Russia is retracing the steps the West has taken over many years along the path to constitutionalism. The courts figure importantly in the evolution toward democracy in several senses. The Constitutional Court will interpret the provisions of any new constitution and is the ultimate arbiter of disputes. The court will help decide how much discretionary power resides with the executive, the limits to and scope for individual rights, and a broad range of electoral issues and disputes between the political branches. The Constitutional Court has asserted, and evidently has acquired, the full right to exercise judicial review. Its jurisdiction, moreover, is not limited to the resolution of specific disputes brought by parties with the appropriate standing. It can intervene on its own in constitutional disputes. Because Russia has historically been a country with a civil code rather than common law, judges have enjoyed great discretion and have been less bound by precedent. The Constitutional Court, even in important cases, has also been less inclined than Anglo-Saxon courts to issue lengthy opinions stating the reasoning behind its decisions.

An interesting feature of the Russian judicial system—reflecting its borrowings from German practice—is that it has a Constitutional Court separate from the regular court system. The regular court system is headed by a Supreme Court. Still another court system, with the High Court of Arbitration at its apex, handles commercial disputes. The complexities of this tripartite system are discussed by Vasily Vlasihin in this volume and were the occasion for animated discussion at the conference. Vlasihin contended that the tripartite system weakened the judiciary and could impede the growth of Russian democracy. Other Russian participants vigorously disputed the contention, some arguing that the division of labor was logical and desirable and others that the dispute was academic and that the nation should get on with the task of making the system work. It will, however, be necesary to establish clear lines of jurisdiction among the various tribunals, define where the lesser tribunals of the Supreme Court and Arbitration Court systems will be located regionally, and relate the work of lesser federal tribunals to the court systems of the regions and localities.

Russian Supreme Court Chief Justice Viacheslav Lebedev, a conference attendee, did not discount the importance of the theoretical issues but emphasized that a great many practical problems need to be addressed before the legal system can function well. These involve the recruitment, appointment, compensation, and training of judges, the efficiency of communications and recordkeeping systems, the adequacy of facilities for subordinate federal tribunals, the effectiveness of mechanisms for enforcing judicial decisions, the relationships between federal and nonfederal court systems, and the relationships between judicial officers and political officials at all levels. Lebedev, the leading advocate of a jury system for Russia, argued that the courts need to be more accessible to the citizens and better supported by them. He noted that the courts are beginning to invoke judicial remedies to curb arbitrary administrative power. He also foresaw a body of case laws emerging to clarify matters such as standing to sue and the enforcement of judicial decrees.

Improving the machinery for making and enforcing laws will place a heavy burden on the legal profession. The judges, on whom so much depends, do not in general have the requisite training, resources, and supporting staff to administer effectively the legal machinery of the new democratic Russia. University law school faculties need training in contract law, commercial law, citizens rights against government, and much more before they can competently teach students in these subjects. Some institutes, such as the Law and Society Institute of the Russian Academy of Sciences, have intellectual talent but lack the facilities and numbers of personnel to handle a large training or educational mission. Creating Western-style law schools within Russian universities and training their professors in free market commercial law and democratic constitutional law will be priorities for the new legal system. A tradition of public attentiveness in the bar associations, law schools, specialized media must also be created. Western legal scholars, law schools, and bar associations should remain actively engaged in working on these problems so that Russian jurists feel they have a supportive collegial group with whom they can confer.

LAW AND THE MARKET ECONOMY

The legal ramifications of economic reform represent a particularly challenging problem. Although frequently overshadowed by the more dramatic political crises, disputes about property law, ownership rights, privatization, and the like are of the utmost importance to the nation's future. Indeed, these disputes frequently trigger the wider-ranging political battles. In virtually every session the conference focused on the relationship between law and economic activity. An initial paper analyzed the laws that have been passed to regulate commercial activity, including those covering direct foreign investment, ownership of property, labor relations, banking practices, energy pricing, and securities transactions. Conference participants attempted to assess the subjects that the legislature has addressed with relative success and those that have not yet been adequately treated. Failure to provide for land ownership was, in the view of most Russian participants, a major stumbing block for attracting foreign investment.

Several American participants questioned whether it was too soon for Russia to attempt to spell out a comprehensive commercial code. The U.S. uniform commercial code, they noted, evolved over many years through thousands of contract interpretations, dispute settlements, and legislative enactments. One tentative suggestion was that Russia might incorporate in whole or in part the German commercial code in lieu of efforts to spell out its own code at this time.

The Russian participants vigorously disputed the observations of their European and American colleagues, arguing that the investment situation is both better and worse than commonly understood in the West. In many sectors entrepreneurial economy has been developing rapidly. Statistics, however, have not been compiled in a useful fashion. Thus the huge drops in production or the soaring inflation rates of an economy not fully monetized give a misleading picture. The technical assistance in drafting legal documents that is provided through international agencies also came in for spirited criticism. Technical assistance is often based, the Russians maintained, on a simplified grasp of conditions and a hasty inclination to prescribe American or European practices.

The conference addressed at length the practical legal problems arising in the conduct of international business activities. John Dealy of Georgetown University noted, for example, that the "due diligence" obligations of corporate directors arising under American law could not always be reconciled with the desires of European partners to name (and hence control) key corporate officers. Dealy observed that a complex new pattern of business interactions is emerging in the global economy that will redefine legal concepts as well as corporate governance practices. As ventures with Russian business firms grow in number and complexity, the law will have to evolve accordingly. Dealy and others emphasized that the capacity of the court system to enforce contractual obligations was the sine qua non for business expansion.

Robert Cooter's paper on the ownership rights of organizations sparked a lively debate among conference participants on how to bring the intersection of law and economics into clear focus. Cooter considered corporate ownership rights the crucial property right for the new Russia. Russians must be able to own, sell, rent, lease, or otherwise dispose of their shares in a company, and owners must be able to replace inefficient managers if the virtues of a market economy are to be realized. Under the Stalinist dictatorship, he said, Russia was virtually the property of Stalin. Later it exchanged such totalitarian ownership for a looser political method of property allocation under bureaucratic communism. Now it is struggling toward the greater efficiencies of market-based ownership and free disposal of property rights.

The regulation of Russia's nascent banking system and the financial dimensions of the market economy stimulated an intricate discussion. Gordon Getty set the framework. Starting with the proposition that commercial banks are inherently prone to failure because of their high ratio of overhead to assets, he sought a way for the new Russia to leapfrog the slow evolution of Western banking practices by means of a system based on mutual funds. Shares of mutual funds could be convenient units of exchange and could substitute for some of the conventional uses of money while providing insurance against bank failures, financial panics, and the like.

In his commentary on Getty's paper, Robert Litan said he believed the proposal was more applicable to conditions in advanced Western economies than in Russia. Many businesses might not be large enough to issue stock or own enough shares of a mutual fund to provide working capital. Some Russians were intrigued with Getty's proposal and noted that financial mechanisms similar to the ones he suggested were emerging in various regions.

Conference participants uniformly agreed that direct manipulation of monetary policy by the legislature was highly undesirable and in the long run incompatible with stable macroeconomic policy.

FEDERALISM AND DEMOCRACY

Achieving a working federal system will be one of the greatest challenges to the new Russia. Already regions, states, and localities have achieved considerable autonomy, and centralized control of resources and domination of policymaking have all but disappeared. These have in many respects been healthy developments: even shorn of its outlying republics, Russia remains a vast and diverse land. In the nature of things its size defies rigid central rule. At the same time, a working federalism requires a strong center of gravity.

In the United States the separation of powers among the executive, legislative, and judiciary at the federal level is replicated at the state and again (in most instances) at the local level, creating both a division of powers and a sharing of functions in virtually every aspect of government policy and administration. It took years to determine the powers of the federal government to preempt local action, enforce uniformity of treatment for the interstate flow of goods, and ensure the "full faith and credit" of laws across different jurisdictions. And conflicts of laws, of course, continue to arise and pose acute problems.

Russia's problems of adjustment will be vastly more complex. Many of the most important issues of federalism reflect unsolved problems and executive-legislative conflicts that must be confronted. Until and unless the disputes between President Yeltsin and his parliamentary critics can be resolved, the powers of the autonomous republics, regions, territories, and localities cannot be sorted out. The fear of forcing Yeltsin into too close an alliance with regional leaders may persuade some deputies to be more accommodating in ratifying the constitution. However, increased regional power has already developed a strong momentum and has become perhaps the most sensitive issue in the ratification process. Yeltsin's draft constitution gives the ethnic republics, led by Tartarstan, special concessions to keep them within the federation, including the right to adopt their own constitutions, anthems, and flags.[11] In response to those concessions, Yakaterinburg, Vladivostock, and Krasnoyarsk-Irkutsk, three of the richest and most powerful provinces, threatened to proclaim themselves, respectively, the Republic of the Urals, the Maritime Republic, and the East Siberian Republic. The drafting and ratification processes will have to reconcile these claims. The task will be to devise some system of integration and enough common direction so that the federation does not fly apart into a large number of new and squabbling independent states.

President Yeltsin has been a stronger advocate of regional and local control than his critics in the Congress of People's Deputies, many of whom wish to reassert strong central control, and he has consistently endorsed the further devolution of powers. As early as October 6, 1992, in a speech to the Supreme Soviet, he stated:

> The center of reform is now being shifted to the regional level. This approach has to be strictly adhered to in drawing up the 1993 budget as well. The regions' share in the budget has to be increased. I regard the delay of the process of transfer of power to local regions as a highly negative factor. Without delegating a large share of the rights of the federal government to the regions, the reforms will skid off course. There are a number of ministries which espouse decentralization in words while in their deeds they stubbornly hold on to the idea of commanding Russia only from Moscow. It is time to say goodbye to this administrative approach once and for all. The role of the federal level is to develop unified notions of the development and location of the productive forces of the country and provide uniform incentives; all the rest is up to the regions. If they are given freedom to maneuver, the economy will begin an upswing.[12]

This expression apparently still represents his attitude toward federalism. Undoubtedly, a complicated pattern of political loyalties has also influenced him. Regional and local authorities have been allies in his battles with the legislature, but the centrifugal forces of regionalism may eventually pose a more serious threat to the federation than a hostile legislature.

It is difficult to get a clear grasp on how much autonomy regional and local authorities have been granted, or have simply seized. Recent economic statistics on *oblast*-level activities show striking contrasts in

inflation rates, economic growth, and other indicators among the regions. Moscow and St. Petersburg are near the bottom for many indicators; they have, for example, experienced the largest declines in real
wages and profits. The vote on the April 1993 referendum illustrated
other striking regional differences and potential signs of trouble. Moscow and St. Petersburg overwhelmingly supported Yeltsin, but some
autonomous republics registered large margins against the president
and his program and a few chose not to participate in the referendum.
This contrast in economic performance and political outlook suggests
some of the strains that the federation will face.

Entrepreneurs who seek to be active across all of Russia need uniformity of treatment within some broad limits. The protection of industrial standards, clear rules of commerce, enforcement of contracts,
and free movement of goods and capital must be maintained even as
local taxation, regulations, and public-private sector cooperation vary
among the regions. Their commercial rights are as important as basic
human rights, civil liberties, and checks on arbitrary power, which
also require national protection. A hierarchical system of courts will
be crucial both to resolving commercial disputes and to protecting
political rights.

POLITICAL PARTIES

The key to making Russian democracy work in the long run lies with
the political parties. Russia is in the difficult position of having a
nomenklatura from the old regime, a few visible democratic leaders, a
weak but developing judiciary, and a highly developed mass media,
but virtually no organized, modern political parties. After the August
1991 coup attempt, there were more than one hundred parties (the old
Duma parties simply resurfacing after seventy years of communism).
Two years later this number had shrunk to about forty. The system is
apparently contracting to a left bloc, a right bloc, and a large center
bloc (itself a collection of dozens of parties covering a wide ideological
spectrum). But none of the parties is a real party in either the contemporary U.S. or the European sense. They are mostly narrow groups
of notables and intellectual followers. Only a few have much of a mass
base. Strong roots in the electorate will have to come before a stable
political dialogue can develop.

For a time President Yeltsin appeared to govern above parties in the fashion of Charles de Gaulle, Dwight Eisenhower, or Winston Churchill (as leader of a wartime coalition government). Yeltsin has, however, decided to create a political party, assigning his first prime minister, Yegor Gaidar, the role of party builder and organizer.

But one should perhaps not oversell the idea that the only "modern" party is large and mass based in the fashion of the British Labour party or the German Social Democratic party. American and Japanese parties have never followed the European model. Instead, they have been loose agglomerations of disparate groups with weakly developed linkage to the broad public.[13] In this respect, as with internal administrative and institutional arrangements, the well-established democracies offer no single or simple recipe for Russia to follow.

Russia should resist efforts to establish proportional representation systems at the various governmental levels. These systems have a seductive appeal; all groups can achieve some degree of representation at once and thus feel democratically empowered. But paralysis often results. Building stable majorities and coherent oppositions becomes more difficult. That is why Italy, Denmark, Holland, and Belgium seem to be reexamining their electoral systems. They attribute tendencies toward factionalism and instability in part to their proportional representation systems.

Critics of single-member districts and "first past the post" elections (those that can be won with a plurality of the vote) object that, with large numbers of candidates running, it is possible for a candidate to win an election with a low vote percentage. A runoff among the top several candidates can, however, largely remedy this problem. Various kinds of electoral lists schemes, as practiced in Germany, can also be employed to strengthen the parties. Campaign finance provisions can be framed to strengthen party organs as well (party financing in America weakens the power of party organizations because candidates raise most of their own funds). Major decisions on electoral law will be made in the context of the debate on the constitution, and the next round of elections will be held in conformance to the new constitution. The important decisions will include the extent of the president's independence, the composition of the upper house (which will be appointed rather than directly elected), the boundaries of electoral districts and the voting rules for the lower house, and party finance.

CONCLUSION

The new Russia has made remarkable progress toward democracy in a very short time, but many obstacles remain. The perplexity of observers who attempt to assess the state of law and democracy in Russia is reflected in the title of Donald Barry's recent volume, *Toward the "Rule of Law" in Russia?*[14] The concept of the rule of law is in quotation marks because the Russian term *pravovoye gosudarstvo* (a law-governed state) has been almost drained of meaning in current Russian political debate. All factions subscribe to the concept, but give it diverse interpretations. The contributors to the volume disagree about how far, or even whether, Russia has moved away from the Soviet concept of law as simply the ordinances, rules, decrees, and statutes adopted by the various state organs. Confusion existed before 1989 about the hierarchy of those measures operating as laws—there were no clear statutes passed by a parliament that could then constrain the behavior of administrative agencies. Similarly, Russia today faces uncertainty over what is the binding "law" to be enforced by the courts, because the legitimacy of the legislature is in dispute, as is the scope of presidential power. The question mark in Barry's title suggests the lack of agreement among the volume's contributors on whether Russia is moving firmly, haltingly, or not at all toward stable democracy.

The obstacles that confront the new Russia lie chiefly in the weakness of the political institutions and practices that give direction and coherence to governmental activity. Russia has experienced, in extreme form, its own version of the political gridlock that has afflicted other democracies. In Russia's case, however, gridlock has meant more than sluggish economic growth, budget deficits, and an inability to formulate new policies. Russian economic output has declined, not merely grown slowly (though the shadow or informal economy has grown dramatically). Inflation has spiraled toward hyperinflation, and political paralysis has threatened permanent crisis. But we must view the situation in perspective. Those who deplore the government's failure to act and yearn for a return to order mistake the nature of democracy. Yeltsin could act without constraint only if the democratic spirit unleashed by *glasnost, perestroika*, and the quest for *pravovoye gosudarstvo* had been choked off. The imaginary efficiency of a conflictless regime should recall the stagnation of the Brezhnev era.

Democracy is a boisterous and clamorous human activity. Disorder, policy zigs and zags, and rambunctiousness are to be expected as energies are liberated, people acquire the right to self-expression, and the fear bred by totalitarianism disappears. The appropriate U.S. stance should not be hectoring but supporting as Russia seeks to devise the political, judicial, and governmental institutions that will give reality to its new democratic order.

As this volume goes to press the constitutional struggle between President Yeltsin and his parliamentary opponents continues. The most dramatic and momentous events since the attempted coup of August 1991 have been unfolding, and no one can predict the outcome. The protagonists appear to be indulging in histrionics, yet they have repeatedly backed off from a final confrontation.

On July 12, 1993, the conference called by Yeltsin formally approved the draft of a new constitution, but rivalries among Russia's provinces and autonomous republics threatened early adoption. The Congress of Peoples' Deputies, though on the defensive since the April referendum, continued to insist on its right to amend and finally approve any new draft. But the events seem to point toward early elections and adoption. Should this prove true, Russian democracy will have reached an important milestone. In any event the nation has bought time and continues to progress toward a pluralist politics in which the president and legislature, however uneasily, at least coexist. The confidence Russians would gain through successfully resolving their gridlock could at last also begin to produce the stable conditions required for economic expansion.

NOTES

1. Joseph A. Schumpeter, *Capitalism, Socialism, and Democracy* (London: Allen and Unwin, 1952); and Samuel P. Huntington, *The Third Wave: Democratization in the Late Twentieth Century* (University of Oklahoma Press, 1991).

2. R. Bruce McColm, *The Comparative Survey of Freedom 1991–1992: Between Two Worlds* (New York: Freedom House, 1992), p. 47.

3. Charles Howard McIlwain, *Constitutionalism: Ancient and Modern* (Cornell University Press, 1977).

4. See Donald D. Barry, "The Concept of the Law-Governed State and Soviet Legal Reform," in Alfred J. Rieber and Alvin Z. Rubinstein, eds., *Perestroika at the Crossroads* (Armonk, N.Y.: M. E. Sharpe, 1991), pp. 137–38.

5. Ibid. See also John N. Hazard, "The Evolution of the Soviet Constitution," in Donald D. Barry, ed., *Toward the "Rule of Law" in Russia? Political and Legal Reform in the Transition Period* (M. E. Sharpe, 1992), pp. 102–11; and John N. Hazard, William E. Butler, and Peter B. Maggs, *The Soviet Legal System: The Law in the 1980's* (Dobbs Ferry, N.Y.: Oceana Publications, 1984).

6. See Dietrich A. Loeber, "Legal Rules 'For Internal Use Only,' " *International and Comparative Law Quarterly*, vol. 70 (1970), p. 19.

7. See Barry, "Concept of the Law-Governed State," p. 138; and Eugene Huskey, "From Legal Nihilism to *Pravovoe Gosudarstvo*—Soviet Legal Development, 1917–1970," in Barry, ed., *Toward the "Rule of Law" in Russia?* pp. 31–33.

8. See John M. Gaus, *Great Britain: A Study in Civic Loyalty* (University of Chicago Press, 1929); Sidney Verba, *Civic Culture Revisited* (Newbury Park, Calif.: Sage Publications, 1989); and Gail W, Lapidus, "State and Society: Toward the Emergence of Civil Society in the Soviet Union," in Sewereign Bialer, ed., *Politics, Society, and Nationality inside Gorbachev's Russia* (Boulder, Colo.: Westview Press, 1989), pp. 121–47.

9. See the discussion of this point in Harold J. Berman, "The Rule of Law and the Law-Based State with Special Reference to the Soviet Union," in Barry, *Toward the 'Rule of Law' in Russia?* pp. 43–60. See also Donald D. Barry, "The Quest for Judicial Independence," in ibid., pp. 257–75.

10. The Constitutional Court had ruled that the two propositions on the ballot pertaining to elections required a majority of all registered voters. Although this turnout was not achieved, voters unmistakably expressed disapproval of the congress and indicated a desire for early congressional elections.

11. Serge Schmemann, "Constitutional Conference Backs Draft of New Russian Constitution," *New York Times*, July 13, 1993, p. A2.

12. TASS version of Yeltsin speech to the Supreme Soviet, October 6, 1992. I am indebted to Clifford G. Gaddy for this quotation and translation.

13. See Gerald Curtis, *The Japanese Way of Politics* (Columbia University Press, 1987); and A. James Reichley, *The Life of the Parties: A History of American Political Parties* (Free Press, 1992).

14. See note 5.

WOLFGANG FIKENTSCHER

From a Centrally Planned Government System to a Rule-of-Law Democracy

This paper first addresses a philosophical issue of value judgments. I want to contrast doubt and dialogue on the one hand with dogmatism and "correct" consciousness on the other. From this contrast everything else follows. The second section deals with the institutional issues of a rule-of-law democracy; the third section develops the implications of the previous discussion for law enforcement; and the fourth deals with what is called in Germany *soziale Marktwirtschaft* (literally, social market economy), which is the economic corollary to democratic political institutions. Finally, I make some practical proposals for economic liberalization and for political liberalization in Russia and the former communist bloc.

DOUBT AND DIALOGUE VERSUS DOGMATISM AND "CORRECT" CONSCIOUSNESS

This necessarily brief survey of the requirements for a free democratic and economic society must start with values. There are only two ways to ascertain values. Either one starts from the premise that a human being cannot know exactly what is true, good, or beautiful, so that there must be a dialogue about the correctness of his or her judgments. Or else somebody says, I know what truth, justice, and beauty are. There is no dialogue. The dictator, for example, attempts to prescribe the thinking of his subjects on truth, justice, and aesthetics, and insists on a correct consciousness.

Organized dialogue about value judgments has a name—democracy. Democracy starts from the legitimacy of the doubt about ultimate values. The political form of the enforcement of preconceived knowledge and correct consciousness has already been mentioned: a totalitarian dictatorship.

That value judgments in the political and economic arena are possible only on the basis of either dialogue or enforced preconceived notions has far-reachng effects. *Democracy* is the organized dialogue on politically relevant values. If the values in question are economic rather than political, the organization of this economic dialogue is a *market*, or a free market process. Inasmuch as the dialogue on political value judgments is the essence of democracy, and the dialogue on economic value judgments the essence of the market, in a given human society democracy and the free market system cannot be separated. Democracy and free trade go together because they both stem from dialogues on value judgments.

Equally, politically enforced value preconceptions apply to economic as well as political issues. That is the essence of Marxism. Marx started on the economic side. He distrusted values in the market place, which he derided as exchange values. An economy based on exchange values was necessarily exploitative because it implied the creation of surplus values that were in turn appropriated by the owners of the means of production. Instead, Marx insisted on a true value for every item of merchandise and service, called use value. The use value is inherent in everything, but to make it economically operational it had to be specifically prescribed by a central economic planning administration.

As soon as use values are subjected to dialogue and criticism, they become by definition exchange values. On the other hand, use values, prescribed by the political authority, are beyond any debate and dialogue. Therefore a Marxist economy could be realized only in the political form of a dictatorship. Since no one was permitted to doubt the correctness of prescribed values, authoritarianism could readily harden into totalitarianism.

The People's Republic of China wants to combine centralized political leadership with a decentralized market economy. This can work only if political and economic value judgments can be separated in the minds of the Chinese population. Such a separation would be in contradiction to the Confucian mode of thought that sees everything connected with everything. The Chinese approach is doomed to failure, and one can expect either a return to ideological centralization or a capitalist-style economic development to gradually emerge.

Dialogue takes time. This applies to political decisionmaking and to economic decisionmaking. The time spans used may be longer or shorter, but time is always involved. So is history. Preconceived knowledge is timeless. Politically prescribed value judgments lack the time dimension and the contingent element of history. Thus Karl Marx was correct when he said that there was a history up to now, but that from now on there is no history. The stagnation that took place in the Soviet Union between the 1917 October Revolution and the USSR's demise in our time reflects both the fact and the perception, behind the Iron Curtain, that Marxism had removed the socialist camp from the dynamic forces of history.

Thus the communist bloc came to an end for mainly two reasons. First, having an economy with use values simply became too expensive in the long run. There were no cost controls in the system. Yvzey Liberman, a great Russian economist and professor in Kharkov, pointed this out in the 1960s. The central planning authority in Moscow, Gosplan, thereupon made an effort to introduce world market costs—that is, exchange values—into its pricing structure.[1] But Gosplan could never quite catch up with, nor did it wish to embrace, price trends in Western markets. In 1980 the Soviet Union joined the Restrictive Business Practices Code, the United Nations agreement on a worldwide competitive order, once again partly accommodating to Western practices and market pricing mechanisms. This led to the contradiction that the communist bloc was living under a system of use values—politically determined prices set by Gosplan—while attempting to participate in the world economy, which operated under an exchange, or market, system.

The resulting problems were the second main reason for the mounting economic troubles of the communist bloc—and which gave rise to *perestroika* in Russia in the second half of the 1980s as an effort to resolve the economic crisis of communism. The consequence of living partly under exchange, partly under use values was particularly felt in East Germany. A colleague in business law in East Berlin sadly remarked to me at the time: "Socialism is a good thing. But it is simply too expensive."

The breakdown of the communist bloc and the realization that Marxism in practice implies totalitarianism poses the problem for eastern European countries of the transition from their centrally planned systems to democracy, with all the attendant legal and economic complexities.

A major difficulty with the transition is that the failure of Marxism does not bring the world any nearer to the solution of what is called the social question. The demands of social justice will have to be kept in mind as ways are found to make the transition. And of course more questions are involved than just the social one. The rule of law, its enforcement, and the establishment of markets as frameworks for dialogues on economic values and on everything that belongs to such markets have to be considered.

DEMOCRACY AND THE RULE OF LAW

The term "rule of law" is used here in the sense of the German term *Rechtsstaat*.[2] Under the rule of law the citizen can insist on his or her rights, both against the state itself and against his or her fellow citizens. To guarantee the rule of law, or *Rechtsstaat*, two elements are necessary: the separation of governmental power and the right to sue the state. Western democracies customarily exhibit formally in their written or informally in their unwritten constitutions a tripartite division of powers: legislative, judicial, and administrative. The three control one another and form a system of checks and balances. By contrast, communism is built on a unity and hierarchy of powers, with the institutional structure ultimately ruled by a single party that has a monopoly on power. The tripartite structure of democracy is not in itself the critical variable; the important thing is the *division* of powers. The Republic of China (Taiwan) possesses five governmental powers (the three Western ones plus education and control). The Tewa-speaking pueblos in northern Mexico count no less than eight governmental powers that control one another. Mutual control is the point, not the number of functional branches of government.

The rule of law is the first and most important protective mechanism for the citizen in a democracy. In particular, it guarantees the rights of minorities. Essential to a democracy is protection for all kinds of minorities. Democracy starts from the premise that some values are absolute and are therefore safe from majoritarianism. Three kinds of minority rights are worth mentioning here.

First is the right of a minority in a democracy to have the freedom to challenge the existing majority and acquire power through persuasion. Nobody can claim to know the absolute truth. So to be able to make wise political decisions, a democracy takes decisions by majorities that are valid for only a given span of time. That for a certain time the majority gives leadership to one group is sometimes called, by critics of the democratic system, the dictatorship of the majority. In reality, this is not a dictatorship but the mandate of the electorate to govern. Of course, the right of the majority to decide is acceptable only for a fixed period, and under the condition that the next time the minority will have a fair chance to become the majority. Therefore the most important right of the minority is the right to become the majority.

Second is the right of the *smaller unit* against the larger unit. Roman Catholic social theory has developed the so-called principle of subsidiarity.[3] This principle teaches that every decision should be made by the smallest unit, and that the decision of the sub-unit must be respected by the higher units of political authority. According to this theory, human society is organized from the bottom to the top and not vice versa. What can be decided in the village square should be decided there. What the district can decide should be respected by the nation-state, and what the state decides has to be accepted by the federation. In Germany, this right is a claim that can be raised in court. The principle of subsidiarity is a healthy presumption for every federation.

Third and most important are *human rights*. The individual in a sense is a minority that needs protection for his or her humanity against capricious or malevolent state action. The rule of law provides for these human rights within the jurisdiction of the state, but in a sense these rights are given to everyone in the world (and as such are properly called human rights). The right of habeas corpus is one of these basic rights. Whenever only nationals of a sovereign country enjoy these rights (for example, the right to freely form associations), the term "civil right" or "basic right" may be preferred to "human right."

These basic human and civil rights are protected against violation by the state. By contrast, in communist countries rights serve as an instrument for the development of the communist society. With this orientation the concept of a right loses its meaning. Human and basic rights can also affect relations between private persons, and they give shape and content to underlying principles of private and other laws.

This is not the place to discuss human rights in detail. For a democracy, however, such rights are of decisive importance. Sometimes it is said that democracy is the rule of the majority, period. But such a notion is incompatible with the rule of law in its fullest sense. Only 50 percent plus one would enjoy full rights under an absolute majoritarianism. In a democracy the other 50 percent have inalienable rights that cannot be taken from them by any temporary majority.

Any democracy is a unit composed of sub-units. There are rights and duties running up and down and within and between the units. The various units may be guaranteed by the constitution. Constitutions can be revised, however. In times of change, uncertainty may cloud the existence and the extent of the claims among the sub-units. One thing is certain, however: not only must democracy tolerate sub-units, but it exists by virtue of such sub-units. A sub-unit that finds its claims respected and taken into consideration is more likely to feel free and to stay within the democratic framework.

Cultural and ethnic diversity is a broad field. It covers large numbers of difficult aspects, and space permits only a few remarks here. Several situations should be distinguished:

—Biculturality can refer to ethnically distinct territorial units within a larger polity or political jurisdiction. Biculturality in this sense happens mainly for historical reasons, such as intermarriages of nobility, expansionist wars, and separation of countries as a result of a lost war. In central Europe, the Slovenes in Austria and the Austrians in northern Italy are classic instances. The Serbs in Croatia and the Turks in Bulgaria serve as further examples.

—Biculturality or multiculturality can also refer to situations in which ethnically, religiously, or otherwise culturally different parts of the population live interspersed throughout the country or within the same area. The Turkish *Gastarbeiter* in Germany and the African Americans in the United States are appropriate examples. The Serbs, Croatians, and Muslims in Bosnia illustrate a multicultural situation that was successful until the tragic events of the past year. The interspersed settlement may be caused by political design and strategy—the Russians in Estonia, the Sicilians in south Tyrol, the African Americans in the United States—or by one group that more or less voluntarily moved into the area of another. The cultural mix may, finally, be the result of a long and unique pattern of historical development.

—A third situation is the cultural enclave, such as an Indian reservation in the United States or Canada.

The interests that have to be protected under the rule of law differ in these different types of bi- and multiculturality. There may be also other, lesser-known types. Mutual understanding and tolerance and much well-designed law will be required to find widely acceptable solutions for the many legal, economic, and religious problems that arise in such diverse societies. Nonacceptability may become the cause for migration movements.

LAW ENFORCEMENT

Nobody objects to lofty principles such as the rule of law, religious liberty, and freedom of speech. In the process of democratization, however, the importance of a workable law enforcement policy is often overlooked. Under Franco, Spain was regarded as a "safe country." Oral tradition has it that every thief got six years in jail, whether it was an armed street robbery or the simple theft of a chicken from a neighbor's courtyard. The crime rate was low. After Franco's death in 1975, in the pursuit of rapid democratization Spain committed the mistake—and other countries followed suit—of reducing the efficiency of the police and of "liberalizing" its system of criminal law. This well-intentioned but ill-advised relaxation brought about a dramatic increase in the crime rate, including Mafia activity. Experience teaches that the beginning of the democratization process in former dictatorships may lead to an abuse of newly won liberties. This need not be so. Spain has taken effective steps to cure these ills.

Democracy does not entail the creation of a permissive atmosphere for crime, or laxness in investigating and prosecuting it. True, dictators have survived by declaring dissidents and opposition parties criminals. Once a country turns democratic, opposition parties must be legalized and jailed dissidents freed. But this does not mean that common crime should be legalized or allowed to go unpunished. To tell the one situation from the other, democracy again invokes the principle of doubt and dialogue and rejects preconceived knowledge and correct consciousness. Dissidents and the opposition parties suffered in Spain because they subjected the policy of the dictator to doubt and wanted to open a dialogue. The sooner a fledgling democracy redefines its relationship to crime and revises the inheritance from totalitarianism, the sooner will crime be brought under control and the better for the democracy.

THE SOCIAL MARKET ECONOMY

A 1992 letter to the editor of the *New York Times* outlined a very critical appraisal of the free market system:

> On my visit to the silver mines of Potosi, my guide said eight million died here at the hands of colonial Spaniards and their descendants, who took control of Bolivia's mineral wealth after the 1826 liberation. . . . Thus Bolivians look upon the worldwide movement toward free-market economies with suspicion. The national memory equates private enterprise with unspeakable suffering. Bolivia is not alone. Its neighbors have similarly dark recollections of a free market at its most wanton. It was only in 1964 that Ecuador shed the dreaded "wasipungo" system.[4]

Noboby wants such a "free market." But what is wrong with the Bolivian and many other "free market systems"? Does market always mean exploitation? How should the forces of the free market systems be harnessed, regulated, or restricted? The solution to the riddle is to be found not in a rejection of the market but in an understanding of its requirements.

A "market" requires several elements: a good (merchandise or service), an area, and a time frame.[5] In a market at least two parties compete for the favor of a third (who will normally be a buyer or a supplier), knowing that only one can succeed. This is the essence of competition. The buyer will choose the better good or service or the more handy one, the more friendly supplier or the quicker or cheaper one. The unfit, the more costly, or the slower seller or supplier will lose. It is the working of the invisible hand. In short, a functioning market will be the most effective distributor of scarce goods. Let me emphasize the word *functioning*.

In a functioning market, only the fittest survive. But this gives rise to a paradox. The market ceases to exist if only the monopolist is left. The market has, in a sense, abolished itself. The market must not be permitted to do so. Thus we are confronted with what may be called the freedom paradox, a political expression of which is the liberty to elect a dictator. The Germans did this in 1933 when Hitler's terror helped to abolish what was left of the Weimar Republic. Hence the Germans have become specialists in the freedom paradox and secured the essentials of democracy in Article 79 of their Constitution by making it impossible to elect a dictator.

For the same reason, the Germans have a strict antimonopoly law: economic freedom must not lead to its own abolition. The free market is safeguarded against the freedom paradox. And it is noteworthy that the Germans regard this competition policy as essential to their social market economy. In Germany, it is considered appropriate that economic influence, gained in the market, is legally subjected to ongoing regulations, scrutiny, and potential redistribution to prevent the rise of monopolies.

The invisible hand generates general utility by the pursuit of the egoisms of the many, but in this general utility there is a counterproductive tendency toward monopoly. Legal safeguarding against this economic freedom paradox is only the general framework of what is "social" in the social market economy. More precisely, what is "social" in such an economy can be grouped into three categories: the social "safety net"; property redistribution; and the establishment of free and fair conditions of trading in the interest of both the entrepreneurs and the consumers (a set of rules that can be called trade regulation, or *Wirtschaftskontrolle*). Furthermore, the important question arises today whether a fourth category should be added: the protection of the environment. I believe the answer is yes.[6]

The social elements of the free market system form constituent parts of an economic order that safeguards the market economy in the long run. Monopolies, such as the Bolivian silver monopoly of Potosi, and exploitative forms of labor market behavior are not inherent or inevitable characteristics of the free market system. The functioning market is the most efficient distributor of the scarce goods, but it needs conscious establishment and care.

The Social Safety Net

Little can be said here about the safety net, important though it is. The participants in the economy are entitled to live with human dignity and to receive help when they are in need. This may involve the apportionment of economic goods that are necessary for survival, such as housing in cities damaged during a war. It may include financial aid if the purchasing power of citizens is insufficient to take care of their most elemental needs. In a social market economy, at least two social elements are seen as preconditions of a functioning market system: a social security system and some degree of social equality or redistribution. In wartime or under similar circumstances, for example, redistribution (*Bewirtschaftung*) is put into effect by a quota or coupon system (*Bezugscheinsystem*). It is a primitive means of economic regulation, seeking nothing more than to divide economic want and suffering. For times of emergency, most countries in Europe have some legislation that permits the speedy enactment of such apportionments (*Sicherstellungsrecht, Notstandrecht*).

Redistribution Mechanisms

The market requires that participants survive and also have a continuing chance for making a new start. Redistribution policies thus go beyond the simple goal of providing for the essentials of life or spreading burdens. They try to give people a new deal by the redistribution of economic opportunities. Again, these redistribution mechanisms are devised to work against some tendencies of the market.

In many European countries, such as Germany, the most important redistribution mechanism is the income tax progression curve. In biblical times one-tenth of a person's income was collected regardless of whether the taxpayer was poor or rich. In a modern state, those who earn more money typically pay not only absolutely but also relatively more tax. In Germany, the maximum tax bracket is 53 percent (including church tax it is 60 percent). This peak is reached at an income of 120,041 deutsche marks, the equivalent of an annual salary of about $80,000. Most enterprises pay this percentage (but not the church tax). A person who earns less than 468 DM per month pays no income tax at all. Between these two points, the income tax moves on a well-rounded curve. Other taxes, for example on property and inheritances, have redistributive effects as well.

There are many other methods of redistribution: rent subsidies, rent regulations, subsidies for young families, subsidies for those who want to begin an independent business, educational allowances, study grants and scholarships for students, and the like. The general idea of these support programs is to assist the underprivileged in order to reestablish, wherever possible, market equilibrium.

Trade Regulation (Wirtschaftskontrolle)

This concept can be defined as the collection of legal measures for the protection of the economy against its own excesses. On the one hand, the social safety net and redistribution primarily concern the correction of the *results* of economic activities. On the other hand, trade regulation has to do with the measures required to keep the economy well functioning over time. Essentially, the freedom paradox in its economic dimension is at issue here. Trade regulation includes antitrust as a key element, but there is more to the concept. Trade regulation, defined broadly, has at least five aspects:

The installation of the market as such. In 1938 Leonhard Miksch published a book called *Wettbewerb als Aufgabe* (Competition as task, as a chore), reprinted in 1947.[7] In a nutshell, this was the program of the Freiburg school of neoliberalism. Miksch thought that the establishment of competition is a duty of the state, something that has to be inaugurated and maintained by the government. This recipe worked for many years after 1948. But following German unification in 1990, too much trust was placed in the so-called self-healing forces of the market. The German government of 1990 had forgotten the teachings of the Freiburg school, so successful in the reconstruction of postwar West Germany, that free markets have to be installed deliberately and carefully built up.

Development and redevelopment of the market. The market runs into trouble whenever it does not function as the most socially oriented distributor of scarce goods. First-aid measures may include the construction of the social safety net and redistribution of the want that the market cannot cure. However, society may also require that the market itself be repaired, reinstituted, or redeveloped. After applying first aid, the real cure must begin. By short-term interventions into the market, its long-term health may be maintained. The benefits of the market system—namely, the most efficient distribution of scarce goods at highest speed to the place of demand and to the greatest possible number—may truly be called a social enterprise. This justifies the governmental task of overcoming market insufficiencies. A housing shortage, for example, may be overcome by subsidized house building. Once there are enough houses and apartments, this sector of the economy may be liberalized again. The planned overcoming of market insufficiencies can also be called development aid. We are used to this term vis-à-vis the third world. Nothing prevents us from also applying the concept to the overcoming of market imbalances within our own economies. These aids, usually granted in the form of subsidies, are not meant to be permanent, but are supposed to cease once the economic sector concerned recovers.

Competition policy. A free market needs protection against distortion. This is the first of several tasks of classical antitrust law. Where there are agreements with the intent or the effect of preventing or restraining competition, such agreements must be prohibited and their effects repaired. In this context, the investigation and policing of horizontal cartels and similar arrangements is to be distinguished from the evaluation of trade restraints in connection with vertical distribution strategies.

Merger control. A subfield of classical antitrust law deals with the prevention of market distortion in the first place. Merger control is a prominent example of such ex ante regulation. It is in the area of merger control that modern German antitrust law has the greatest number of cases per year. On the international level there is a growing urgency to create a trans-border control mechanism for mergers.[8] In the global economy, legal regulation seems bound to be internationalized as well. Otherwise the egoistic pursuit of profit through the working of the international invisible hand may lead to new and more complex variations of the freedom paradox discussed above.

As if control. Situations remain in which, for a number of practical reasons, functioning markets cannot be established or maintained. In these cases, antimonopoly law steps in by means of what in Germany is called "as if control" (*Als-ob-Kontrolle*). On this point, U.S. antitrust law is less clear. As if control seeks to define the conditions under which tolerated monopolists and trade-restraining oligopolists may function as if they were exposed to competitive forces. They are expected to act competitively (*wettbewerbsanalog*). This means that they have to abstain from collecting what the economists call monopoly rent.[9]

SOME PRACTICAL PROPOSALS FOR
ECONOMIC LIBERALIZATION

Whole libraries exist on how to change a market economy into a socialist centrally planned economy. One can find there the works of many different ideologists: those who rank the political program first, such as the neo-Marxists Ernest Mandel and Rudolph Hickel; democratic socialists like Victor Agartz; pragmatists like Oskar Lange: adherents of a mixed economy like Karl Paul Hensel; theorists of a slow transition from capitalism to socialism like Joseph Alois Schumpeter or Ota Sik. For all of them the world ends sooner or later in socialism. For the opposite development—from a centrally planned economy to a free market economy—until recently almost no book, article, or theoretical study existed.

I believe there are two possible ways to make the transition from a centrally planned to a free market economy. One way is to accept the existing socialist administration as given and to assign to it the tasks and jobs of the transition to a free market economy. This way will run into political opposition, if not obstruction, from the socialist apparatus, which hardly will be enthusiastic about the imposed liberalization. The second way consists in drafting a market-economy model and to derive from it the administrative system needed for its successful adoption. The instruments of former central planning in this conception would be used in a new sense, revamped, or wholly disbanded.

The first way stresses the means, the second the goals. The first is instrumental, the second functional. The functional approach offers the advantage that the necessary debates concentrate on the model of market economy to be followed in the future. My proposal is to follow the second way. This approach uses debate and dialogue, and denies preexisting knowledge and the power of those who pretend to know all the answers in what must inevitably be a contingent and complex endeavor. This way offers the best chance of achieving a rule-of-law democracy, an effective law enforcement and police organization, and a social and environment-oriented market economy (that is, a free economy planned for the long run).

There is no room here to discuss the two substructures indispensable for every market system: a central antitrust authority able to control economic power and an independent central bank that guarantees a stable currency. The transition to a free economy implies both a viable competitive order and the need for real money: money meant to pay exchange values. Stable money and the two other corners of John Maynard Keynes's "magic triangle"—high employment and an equilibrated balance of payments—are critical problems to be solved by the ministries of economy and finance. A competitive order and a stable currency are basic requirements for everything to follow.

How about property ownership and privatization? In the long run, certainly property rights are essential. Without material and intellectual property the market cannot function. But should privatization of property be placed high on the agenda, or should the priorities be given to free prices, a private banking system, or collectively bargained wages? Here, as is well known, the former communist countries have followed different patterns of priority. Freeing prices without the preceding establishment of a competitive system, or privatizing collective property before the establishment of a competitive system, has led to serious difficulties in Russia and elsewhere.

I would suggest the following priority list:

1. It makes sense to begin with free wages. This implies free trade unions, that is, associations of workers in every branch of the economy. These organized labor associations will be accountable to their members for the wages and working conditions achieved in a free collective bargaining process. By collective bargaining, workers necessarily get a feeling for how much their work is worth. For this first step, freely bargained wages, privatization is not necessary. No director of an enterprise, whether state or privately owned, likes collective bargaining. Directors prefer state subsidies. Russia's inflation may have one of its causes right here in the failure of the country's labor laws. This failure was then aggravated by the directors' anticompetitive cartel to rely on subsidies rather than on income earned in the marketplace.

2. If there are wages that may be termed real, there can be savings. This is the beginning of private capital formation. A free banking system can be built around freely bargained wages. Moreover, the capital formation in the hands of the many can be protected and subsidized by the government according to family size, housing needs, and so on. An instrument for doing this is wage tax rebates.

3. A third step is now possible: the formation of private property. Again the government has an important role, and private property becomes meaningful. It is not so much a case of how state enterprises should be privatized, though that will be important. The need is for an overall framework of ownership, including the ownership of land, that will give people the incentive to work and to save, and that will give foreign investors the incentive to supply capital on a large scale.

4. Up to this point, privately or state-run industries have not been of critical importance. Free trade unions, private capital formation, and a competition-minded management come first. For the industries, qualified management is more important than being private. As soon

as possible, a "market for management" should be established. During the first years, this can probably not be done without hired management from abroad. But a market for management is essential for obtaining qualified management.

5. The first four steps describe the formation of private property from the bottom to the top, and not the other way around. Nonetheless, the privatization of public property may parallel those four steps. Investment vouchers are preferable to shares issued to the work force of a given industrial entity. As soon as there are investment papers, or shares, a Western-style stock market is necessary, as well as a stock market law (a securities and exchange commission).

6. Prices should be freed only after a survey, to be made by the ministry of economics, warrants with some certainty that enough merchandise and services will be offered in the marketplace. Otherwise prices will soar. When Germany freed prices after the currency reform of 1948 under Minister of Economics Ludwig Erhard, for example, special care was taken that the supply had enough elasticity to satisfy demand. Price liberalization went sector by sector, the last sectors of the economy becoming price-freed as late as after the Korean War.[10]

SOME PRACTICAL PROPOSALS FOR POLITICAL LIBERALIZATION

As in the economy, in government everything also depends on value judgments. A method does not solve a problem, and a process—whether glasnost and perestroika—does not give rise automatically to political or economic solutions. Deciding a case of law or running an economy inevitably involves the clash of values. Indeed, politics in its essence is the clash of values, and, as noted, values are either preconceived or debated.

Historically, comparatively, and anthropologically, there are three systems of government that are open minded about values; that is, they are built on dialogue. The most ancient governmental forms are kin-metaphors (everybody is a member of some kind of family or kin: brotherhoods, the family boss, the clan mother, and so forth). Use of the kin-metaphor leads to the consensus principle, with its open-minded value-finding.

Some governmental orders use the dual system: Rome, for example, had two consuls. In the Norman kingdoms, power was divided between king and bishop. The Tewa-Moieties are another example.

The most widely spread political order today, however, is the third type, which can be termed the corporate structure. This system was probably invented by the Athenians in the fifth century B.C., and a millennium later independently by the Franks. It has been called "Frankish feudalism." Essentially, I mean here a pledge-of-faith system, in which mutual trust plays an important role. In this system, individual members belong to a unit that is more than the sum of its parts. The members form an assembly and promise one another mutual assistance and trust.[11] Moreover, members then appoint or elect a functionary, an "organ," a "hired power" who is given certain rights to govern, and in turn is accountable after a fixed span of time. The assembly of the members and the administrative unit are also connected by a mutual bond of trust.

The Franks, through this corporate structure of government, became the most successful of the Germanic tribes. They took their pledge-of-faith system to France, the country that adopted their name. There Norman Scandinavians learned it. Some Scandinavians, the Varager, went eastward and formed the Russian nation. Other Normans who had adopted the Frankish pledge-of-faith system took it to England. In England the system grew into modern parliamentarianism, forming the background of many modern constitutions, such as those of Great Britain, the Netherlands, the United States, and Germany. The United Nations was also modeled on a Frankish cooperative. The only Slavic people to introduce the Frankish pledge-of-faith system in Frankish times were the Slovenes. The other Slavic nations applied a type of feudalism, the one-sided variant that gives rights only to the "lord" and mere duties to the "vassals" (members).[12]

Thus the use of the kinship system based on either the consensus principle, the dual principle, or the corporate principle results in the three main forms of government that are not dictatorial or absolutist. All three can fairly be called democratic. Today the most common form is the corporate government, consisting of assemblies and accountable functionaries to handle the day-to-day business of government. Corporate democracies can exist without human rights (such as the ancient Greek city-state based on slavery or the modern so-called totalitarian democracy). But most of the governments that developed from

Frankish feudalism and Christianity have evolved into systems that respect human rights. Human rights democracies can either be direct (Switzerland, the Congregational tradition in the United States) or representative (that is, using delegates in the Presbyterian tradition). Most corporate human rights democracies today are representative. They can be divided into presidential democracies like the United States, and parliamentary democracies like Great Britain or Germany.

The successor states to the Soviet Union and the other countries of the former communist bloc are free to choose from the menu of democratic alternatives. Since Russia is not Slovenia and has never accepted the pledge-of-faith system based on a general assembly and accountable functionaries, I would propose that Russia choose from a mix of the systems just reviewed. Russia cannot neglect the pledge-of-faith system, because most of its friends abroad apply the system in the representative presidential or parliamentarian form. But considering the country's background, the consensus principle and the principle of duality should be given consideration as well. Both principles should be applied in Russia to supplement the modern corporate structure when the latter runs into difficulties.

Under the consensus principle, all have to agree. After 1572 the Poles applied it. Every member of the *Schlachta*, the nobility, could veto a decision; this was called the *liberum veto*. One consequence was that the Poles had to take their kings from abroad, from Russia, Sweden, Austria, Hungary, Saxony, and elsewhere. This in turn resulted in the seemingly endless series of Polish divisions after 1792. The consensus principle may work for a small group, but for a whole country it is too clumsy.

Under the dual system, consensus is required only between the two heads of the respective political sub-units. Each head may represent a group, and it is up to the group how to instruct its head. Dual systems worked for a long time in Uruguay, where two parties took turns in running the country, and in Austria under the unofficial but effective *proporz* system. The two-party system in the United States is a special form of political dualism.

The consensus principle is the most legitimate but the least effective. The corporate democracy, usually a multiparty system, is the most effective democratic form but the least legitimate—since 50.01 percent can outvote 49.99 percent and potentially dominate. The dual system is in between. It is legitimate and still effective enough to get things done. In times of change, doubt, high diversity of opinion, and deeply felt uncertainty, the dual system could be a way out of many troubles. It would conform to Petr Kropotkin's principle of mutual assistance, voiced early in this century.[13]

CONCLUSION

In the first four parts of my paper, I tried to proceed as circumspectly as possible. In the final two parts, I tried to be practical in discussing both economic and political liberalization. My task was not to give advice but to report on possibilities and variations based on observations of comparative law and anthropology. Russia of course must find its own way. But what is at stake is perhaps best summed up by President Boris N. Yeltsin in his January 31, 1992, speech before the Security Council of the United Nations: "Not only the future of the people of Russia but also that of the entire planet largely depends on whether or not the reforms are successful." To that ultimate task it is hoped that these observations may contribute.

NOTES

1. For details of this development, see Wolfgang Fikentscher, "United Nations Codes of Conduct: New Paths in International Law," *American Journal of Comparative Law*, vol. 30 (1982), pp. 577–604.

2. The term "rule of law" has a number of meanings. The following six usages are the most frequent ones: (1) there should be law instead of brute force, that "might should not be right"; (2) historically the king was under, not above, the law of the land, and in modern times the government is subject to the law; (3) a distinction is made between *res publica* and *res privatae*, which ensures that the citizen is entitled to free speech and religious freedom, and that human and other personal rights, the minorities, and the political minority as such are legally safeguarded; (4) rule of law can designate the normative standard that is applicable to decide a case once in court; (5) it can be used in a positivistic concept that excludes justice, so that rule of law is the opposite from a rule of morals, of equity, and so on; (6) similarly, it can be used in opposition to the rule of laws; this amounts to a criticism that a parliament is too busy enacting statutes to look for an overall justice in the government of the country. In this essay, rule of law (*Rechtsstaat*) is used in the third sense.

For another survey, see George P. Fletcher, "Searching for the Rule of Law in the Wake of Communism," *Brigham Young University Law Review* (1992), pp. 145–64.

3. Georg Bernhard Kripp, *Wirtschaftsfreiheit und katholische Soziallehre* (St. Gallen: Polygraphischer Verlag, 1967).

4. Gary D. Rosenberger, *New York Times*, February 22, 1992, p. A-14.

5. This analysis is adapted from Wolfgang Fikentscher, "Free Trade and Protection of the Environment as an Integrated Economic Value System: Outline of an Environment-Conscious Social Market Economy—a Lawyer's View," The 1991 Cassel Lecture, Juridiska fakulteten i Stockholm, *Skriftserien*, no. 34 (Stockholm, 1992), *Juristforlaget*, pp. 15–20.

6. See my discussion in ibid.

7. Leonhard Miksch, *Wettbewerb als Aufgabe, Grundsatze einer Wettbewerbsordnung*, 2d ed. (Godesberg: Küpper, 1947).

8. International Antitrust Code Working Group, "Draft International Antitrust Code—as a GATT-MTO-Plurilateral Agreement" (Munich: Max Planck Institute for Foreign and International Patent, Copyright and Competition Law, 1993).

9. Relevant provisions of the German Act against Restraints of Competition are articles 22; 26 II-1, III-1, 26 II-2, II-3, III-2; 26 IV-5; 38a, 104. Article 86 of the EC Treaty is being interpreted to the same effect.

10. Prices that are freed too early under some sort of shock treatment cause inflation. Another source of inflation in the countries in transition from socialism to the free market system is to be found in the necessary change in the industrial subsidy system. In a socialist economy, there are no real prices. A thorough survey on the problems involved in privatization is given by Christian Kirchner, "Privatization Plans of Central and Eastern European States," *Journal of Institutional and Theoretical Economics*, vol. 148 (1992), pp. 4–19.

11. The *vietche* constitution of historic Novgorod was built on such a (dual) assembly.

12. Rushton Coulborn, ed., with contribution by Joseph R. Strayer, *Feudalism in History* (Princeton University Press, 1956).

13. Petr Alekseevich Kropotkin, *Mutual Aid: A Factor of Evolution* (New York: McClure, Philips, 1902).

VASILY A. VLASIHIN

Toward a Rule of Law and a Bill of Rights for Russia

It is difficult to give a succinct definition of the notion of the rule of law. The concept implies many interrelated themes, such as constitutionalism, separation of powers, a bill of rights under which individual rights and liberties are safeguarded, limited government, an independent judiciary, judicial review, a fair legal order, due process guarantees, and no person being above the law. This list is not exhaustive, of course, but it is my belief that the idea of the protection of rights and liberties of an individual—a bill of rights—constitutes the core of the rule of law.

RECENT STEPS TO IMPROVE THE LEGAL SYSTEM

With the emergence of *perestroika* the idea of the rule of law (*pravovoye gosudarstvo*) made its way into the political vocabulary of Russian society. Once looked upon as an empty bourgeois slogan, the rule of law rapidly became a goal as well as an underlying moral value of *perestroika*. Russian society—battered by the lawlessness of the past and exhausted by the rule-of-state law—initiated a reform of the legal system as a central theme of *perestroika*.

Naturally enough, a country striving for freedom would first try to ensure the most important rights and liberties: freedom of religion, expression, press, assembly, and association, as well as certain procedural guarantees in the system of criminal justice to prevent law enforcement abuses. Constitutional niceties regarding rights and liberties were known, at least in theory, to the Soviet citizenry—they were written into both the Stalin Constitution of 1936 and the Breshnev Constitution of 1977. But those two documents were mere pieces of paper.

It is important to remember that Russia is not a common-law country but a country of statutory law. This means that the contents of individual rights and freedoms are defined not by the Constitution and its authoritative interpretation by the judiciary but by statutes and governmental regulations construing constitutional commands. Before *perestroika*, statutes regarding basic constitutional rights were virtually nonexistent. But there was a huge volume of substatutory governmental regulations (most of which were issued in secrecy and thus were unknown to the public) that "construed" these rights in a restrictive and destructive way. That is why newly elected legislatures moved to adopt statutes that would spell out constitutional rights and liberties. It was thus in the legislature, and not in the courts, that the first important moves toward a bill of rights for the people were made.

Much was done to provide a statutory framework for constitutional rights in the years of *perestroika*. Even after the disintegration of the Soviet Union and the emergence of Russia as an independent state, many Soviet laws affecting rights and liberties that did not contradict the new Russian legislation were left intact and continued to operate in Russia.

A law on the freedom of religion has been one of the most important new laws and has helped to spark the revival of religion in the country. Religious faith is no longer a suspicious trait in a society that under communism was compulsorily atheist. New churches and religious groups have been formed on a wide scale, and Sunday schools are flourishing.

Prompted by the policy of *glasnost*, freedom of expression has blossomed. Criticism of the government has become so widespread that sometimes it seems difficult to find anybody who has something good to say about any government action. Provisions of the criminal code that used to give a free hand to state security organs to prosecute political speech and political dissidents have been revised. Liberty of the press is guaranteed by the law on the press and other mass media. Under that law government censorship is prohibited in absolute terms. Subject to certain regulations, the freedom to assemble is widely used by citizens of different political leanings. Freedom of association is protected in a corresponding statute and has given birth to an assortment of associations, unions, organizations, and political parties. Formerly a one-party society, we have rapidly become a multiparty system.

Russia has also moved to introduce what is known in the United States as due process protections of an individual against abuses by law enforcement and criminal justice authorities. The right to legal counsel is now provided to suspects or defendants at the earliest stages of criminal proceedings. The *Miranda* rule has seemed to sprout even on the hard soil of Soviet-Russian justice. Elements of the jury trial concept are being introduced: serious cases are to be tried by a panel of two judges and three assessors (jurors). Moreover, a movement is afoot to introduce jury trials as they are known in the United States. The leading proponent of the jury system is the energetic and wise chief justice of Russia, Viacheslav Lebedev.

Prosecutorial overzealousness and abuses by law enforcement establishment in most cases do not go unattended: there have been many acquittals by courts and in general there has been close judicial scrutiny of the police and of prosecution evidence. Judges are no longer rubber stamps for government prosecutors.

Important statutes have also been passed to protect the judiciary from infringements on independence—a statute that raises the status of judges and empowers them to issue contempt of court citations. The law provides for civil and criminal penalties for any efforts—political or monetary—to exert pressure on courts. The tenure of judges has been extended to ten years, from five, and future amendments should establish life tenure. Judges' salaries have been greatly increased. The power to nominate and elect judges has been given to higher-level legislators (the reasoning behind this provision being that the process of electing judges by local legislatures might be unduly influenced by narrow local interests and pressures).

Courts have been given extensive powers to provide judicial protection of the rights of citizens against governmental abuses of power. Courts (not bureaucracies as in the past) are now fully empowered to handle complaints of citizens against governmental bodies or officers of any level. Elements of habeas corpus have also been introduced into Russian criminal justice: an arrested person now has the right to challenge in a court the prosecutorial decision to detain.

The Constitutional Court of Russia has been established as a separate single body to exercise constitutional review of legislation and executive or administrative acts. This has been an important step as Russians have sought to effectuate the rule of law system, but one that, as will be discussed, presents problems.

Russia's privately practicing lawyers work within colleges of advocates. Until the end of the 1980s these colleges were tightly controlled by the government and the Communist party. The independence of the bar was almost nonexistent. Indeed, the bar was a stepdaughter of the Soviet legal system, which was largely dominated by the law enforcement and prosecutorial agencies. After the formation in 1989 of a national bar association, the legal profession started to acquire the attributes of a Western bar. Restrictions on attorneys' fees were lifted, attorney-client privilege became inviolable, and colleges of advocates became independent agents in running their businesses.

PROBLEMS WITH THE SYSTEM

I have so far painted a rosy picture of the legal profession and its development in Russia. In reality, despite much progress, we are still very far from achieving the true rule of law. Much has been done, but much more needs to be done. What are the principal roadblocks and obstacles that remain?

Lack of an Appropriate Legal Culture

In my view, the largest roadblock is the lack of the traditions of democracy and constitutionalism and of a genuinely free legal culture.

After a visit to the USSR in 1990, Richard Thornburgh, then the U.S. attorney general, delivered the following remarks in Philadelphia:

What is really missing [in the Soviet Union] is what might be called a "legal culture." Time and again, we found a naive belief that all that was needed was to pass the correct statutes, to get the right laws on the books to create a "rule of law." . . .
It is going to take a commitment to the lawful, democratic process, and we tried to emphasize legal process—due process of law—even over substantive rights, as the true safeguard of the people's liberties.[1]

True, all too many people in Russia think that once you get the right statutes on the books, you automatically create an operative rule of law. But Russians still do not trust law itself: the old Russian saying, "The law is like the shaft of a wagon, it goes wherever you turn it," remains firmly embedded in the public consciousness. This reality simply reflects the past failure of the legal system to provide ultimate protections to the people against government abuses.

Law itself does not yet contain the maximum protection for the citizen against abuses of individual rights and freedoms even with the broadened scope for court action. Most of the vital legal disputes, unfortunately, are still channeled through bureaucratic intermediaries. People do not as yet view courts as their protectors. The bar, by and large, has not yet become—or so it seems to me—a champion of individual rights and liberties.

Many aspects of the rule of law that are widely accepted and understood in the West remain incomprehensible to Russians. The minds of people brought up in the spirit of the rule-of-state law are still incapable of fully absorbing the ideas of limited government, decentralized government, checks and balances and separation of powers, judicial supremacy, and the priority of individual rights and liberties over the interests of the state.

Restricted Freedoms

Closely connected with the lack of an appropriate legal culture is another roadblock, which often results from efforts to limit or license which freedoms can be allowed. In actuality, what we have now in Russia is *the regime of licensed rights and freedoms.*

For example, licenses must be obtained through and from the state in order to start a church, religious organization, newspaper, or magazine. To have a rally or a parade, people must obtain a permit from city authorities. This requirement, of course, is not unknown in the United States or wholly novel in any civilized society. Permits may be necessary to prevent public disorder. But what Russia lacks in issuing a permit is the ability to discriminate between genuine concerns relating to public safety and ideological or political censorship. The Moscow city ordinance on assembly, for example, gives this power to city government officials, along with wide discretionary powers to deny a permit on the speculative grounds of a potential violation of public order.

To start an association or a political party, people have to register with the government. The government is empowered to scrutinize the program, the charter, and the bylaws, and has discretion to deny or allow the registration. Freedom of association is thus unduly licensed.

Glasnost certainly facilitated and liberalized freedom of expression, but it is hard to shake off years of totalitarian traditions and to resist those who would rather preserve the old traditions. *Glasnost* means not only freedom of speech by the citizens but also freedom of information and openness on the part of government. However, the cloak of secrecy still covers many parts of the government machinery. "The right to know" is not yet enjoyed by Russian citizens. We are far from having such laws as the Freedom of Information Act or the Privacy Act.

The potential for the abuse of power by government is still present despite the revision of criminal law provisions that in the past allowed the government to prosecute political dissent. The generally worded article 70 (anti-Soviet propaganda) of the Russian Criminal Code was the main tool of repression in the past. It has been significantly revised. Now the government can prosecute—in theory—only for "public calls for violent overthrow or change of the government and social system, secured by the Constitution."

But, in fact, the code is worded almost exactly as that part of the Smith Act of 1940 in the United States which made punishable "advocacy for violent overthrow of the government." The application of the Smith Act, as punishing "pure speech," was sharply restricted by the standards set by the 1957 Supreme Court decision in *Yates* v. *United States*. And in 1969, in *Brandenburg* v. *Ohio*, the Supreme Court suggested an "imminent lawless action" test as the only valid means to restrict speech. One wonders how long it will take Russian constitutional jurisprudence to develop to that stage inasmuch as it is just now using what in the United States had been written into law in 1940. Built-in statutory devices may tend to chip away newly gained rights and liberties, and the problem is compounded by vagueness in certain statutes. Such standards as "least restrictive means" established by the U.S. Supreme Court would puzzle our legislators.

Certain forms of political speech connected with conduct may require regulation. But our lawmakers, under pressure from law enforcement agencies, try to regulate all speech. In doing so, however, they forget that any regulation can mean control, which in turn can lead to arbitrary restrictions.

The Independence of the Judiciary

A bill of rights can become a living reality only in a democracy where the independence of the judiciary is firmly established, and where the judiciary vested with the power of judicial review is the ultimate guarantor of rights and liberties. Our society does not yet have such a judiciary.

Several features of the judiciary in Russia undermine its proclaimed independence. One important factor is that the courts are organizationally and logistically dependent on the Ministry of Justice, despite the talk about separation of powers and judicial independence. There is a further problem. The constitution proclaims that judges are independent, but at the same time they are obliged to be accountable to the legislative bodies that have elected them.

Moreover, the regular courts are not empowered to exercise judicial review of legislative or executive enactments. Although many argued that at least the Supreme Court of Russia should be vested with this power, the legislature chose instead to create a separate Constitutional Court as the body to judge the constitutionality of statutes and executive actions.

The problem with relying on a single Constitutional Court is that it passes constitutional judgments in disputes that are not based on *actual* cases and controversies (as this is understood in U.S. constitutional law). If, say, some political group does not like a statute or executive act, it may petition the Constitutional Court for a review even if such a statute or act does not inflict *actual injury*. U.S. constitutional standards and requisites of standing require "injury in fact" and "real interest" and preclude "mootness," "abstract issues," and "political question." Such conceptions are foreign to the operational framework of the Constitutional Court of Russia. Furthermore, the establishment of such a court as a tribunal separate from the regular court systems has deprived the judiciary of its most important power—to apply in the administration of justice the fundamental law of the country, that is, its Constitution.

Under the present law, whenever a dispute in a regular court regarding the constitutionality of a statute or an administrative regulation arises, the case must be transferred to the Constitutional Court. That court must then decide the issue of the constitutionality of the "law-applying practice" of a particular court or of a challenged legal enactment. But so far the criteria of "constitutionality" have been vague or nonexistent. Under present law, on the Constitutional Court a petitioner merely has to say that she or he thinks there is a violation of the Constitution. Along with the lack of proper requisites of standing, this arrangement can cause many problems. In view of the vastness of Russia and the size of its population, imagine what would happen to the docket of a single body of constitutional review if citizens start taking their rights seriously and petition the Constitutional Court whenever they think a statute or the "law-applying practice" of a lesser tribunal is unconstitutional. The court will collapse under the weight of its caseload.

A further problem with the ease of petition to the Constitutional Court is the tendency for it to be drawn increasingly into rendering advisory opinions and then into an overt political role. If the court acts without restraint in political disputes, its legitimacy as constitutional arbiter could be eroded. Of course, the U.S. Supreme Court is in some sense "political" as well. The Russian Constitutional Court must not shrink from the great challenge of participating responsibly and creatively as the "life of the law" evolves in Russia and as our new institutions and aspiring democratic politicians confront difficult choices. But these judicial functions are important for *all* courts across the whole country. It is my belief that by not allowing the regular courts to apply and interpret the constitution on their own, the legislature has diminished the roles of the judiciary and made the movement toward the rule of law more difficult.

Another characteristic of the court system also weakens the judicial branch of government: the separation of powers within the court system. In Russia, not all justiciable disputes are handled by the courts. Whenever a dispute arises between business entities, the case is taken for trial by the courts of arbitration (business courts, in fact). But if a party to a case is a private citizen (not involved in business activities), the dispute has to be handled by a regular court. The courts of arbitration are headed by the High Court of Arbitration, which hears appeals from the lower arbitration courts. The articulation of exactly which disputes are to be heard by which category of court is not always clear and will probably become less so as the Russian economy develops and new and complex forms of business arrangements emerge.

Thus the judiciary in Russia is not a single whole; it is split into three branches: the regular court system with the Supreme Court on top, the courts of arbitration system with the High Court of Arbitration on top, and the Constitutional Court as a single body with no courts under it.

This three-prong arrangement poses questions of interjurisdictional relationships. Indeed, can the Supreme Court be regarded as supreme if it is obliged to refer constitutional matters to the Constitutional Court? The chief justice of Russia's Supreme Court is *required* to be present at the Constitutional Court's hearings. It is an oddity that the chief justice is treated as *amicus curiae*, or friend of the court.

CONCLUSION

I believe the future of the court system of Russia lies in merging all courts into a single judiciary, in vesting them with the power of judicial review, in creating an orderly system of lower federal courts sufficient to serve a large federal nation, and in having normal appellate procedures for constitutional litigation. To date, the judicial branch is far from being on an equal footing with the two other branches of government. The judiciary in Russia today is truly "the least dangerous branch."

I have mentioned only the largest roadblocks on the way to an effective rule of law. There are some others. Russia has suffered abuses of the executive power. In the sphere of freedom of speech, the so-called heckler's veto is widespread. The activities of legislatures are sometimes comparable to the early U.S. experiences that have been referred to as "legislative tyranny." In the summer of 1992, for example, the Russian parliament sought to curb the press by establishing an oversight committee. Finally, police misconduct is all too common.

But once fear is gone, hope is there.

Russia is now in the process of drafting its new constitution. The part of the draft that deals with rights and liberties of citizens is worded so that it resembles a bill of rights in a civilized democracy. The provision refers to natural and inalienable rights and asserts that the liberty of a human being is of the highest value.

The moves to ensure constitutionalism make me feel optimistic. The Romans had a relevant maxim, *Per aspera ad astra*—through difficulties, through thorns, to the stars. In Russia we are now moving painfully through a political thornbush. But we are not just scratching ourselves. We finally see the stars.

NOTE

1. "The Rule of Law in the Soviet Union: How Democracy Might Work," remarks by Richard Thornburgh, Attorney General of the United States, before a luncheon meeting of the World Affairs Council of Philadelphia, press release, U.S. Department of Justice, April 4, 1990.

ROBERT D. COOTER

Organizational Property and Privatization in Russia

Russians who immigrate to the United States dramatically increase their productivity as soon as they take jobs in American industry. The large difference in productivity between the United States and Russia apparently results from the organization of industry, not from the character of the work force. Industry is organized by practice and law. In this paper I consider the legal foundation of capitalist organization. The Ford Motor Company is the same thing in law as I am, specifically a legal person. Furthermore, the Ford Motor Company can be owned, just like I own my toothbrush. I will explain how these facts promote the efficiency of the U.S. economy.

Most production in modern economies occurs in organizations, which come in many forms such as corporations and partnerships. Ideally, private property and capitalism provide a framework for competition among these forms of organization. The most productive ones should flourish in a capitalist environment and the less productive ones should disappear. The legal ideal of capitalism is neutrality of law toward forms of organization.

In practice, however, fundamental differences in organization, especially in the way leaders are chosen and dismissed, result from differences in law and public policy. For example, management in public corporations faces the possibility of hostile takeovers in America but not in Germany or Japan. The difference is a consequence of law, not competition. In sum, there are many capitalisms, not just one.

This last observation raises questions about the limits of the law's neutrality in the competition among organizational forms. Are private

A longer version of this paper, entitled "Organization as Property: Economic Analysis of Property Law and Privatization," appeared in Christopher Claque and Gordon Rausser, eds., *The Emergence of Market Economies in Eastern Europe* (Blackwell, 1992), pp. 77–97.

property and capitalism incomplete until law and policy favor particular forms of business organization? Or can private property and capitalism provide a neutral framework for competition among enterprises with different forms of organization?

This paper seeks to answer these questions by applying the concept of property, as developed in the economic analysis of law, to markets for organizations. I conclude that imperfections in markets for corporate control preclude pure neutrality of the law. This conclusion has an important implication for privatization in eastern Europe. Russia must choose among the several capitalisms when developing a legal framework for corporate control. The United States, Germany, and Japan offer alternative models, although the post-communist countries will probably develop their own hybrids.

A PURE PROPERTY REGIME

Property is the institution that gives people discretion over scarce resources. Discretion is created by assigning rights to owners and prohibiting others from interfering with their exercise. Rights convey upon owners the legal power to act or forbear, without imposing the obligation to do either. Owners are not legally bound to answer to others, whether private persons or public officials, about how they exercise their property rights unless they have voluntarily assumed such obligations by contract. By surrounding owners with discretion, property creates a zone of privacy within which they can do as they please.[1]

I use the phrase *a pure property regime* to refer to a body of law that creates full and complete rights of ownership and protects them from interference. A conventional list of full and complete property rights includes the right to use, consume, deplete, destroy, improve, develop, transform, sell, donate, bequeath, mortgage, or lease the resource. Full and complete protection from interference by private persons or governments includes prohibitions against trespass, invasion, theft, destruction, nuisance, pollution, flooding, unauthorized use, appropriation, expropriation, takings, and nationalization. Violation of the owner's rights might result in liability for past harm, injunction against future recurrences, or criminal punishment.

How large should the owner's zone of discretion be? An owner enjoys the most discretion when he or she can do anything with his or her resources that does not harm others. In economic terms, the law maximizes the owner's discretion subject to the constraint that its exercise does not cause harm to anyone. I call this proposition the *principle of constrained maximum discretion*.

Causing harm is a necessary condition for legal liability in most circumstances. But since people and nature form such a complex ecology of interdependence, determining who harmed whom is problematic. Social and legal norms stipulate what counts as causing harm to others. To illustrate, charging a monopoly price harms buyers and often results in liability under antitrust law. In contrast, bidding down the price of a good in a competitive market harms other suppliers but does not ordinarily result in liability. The relevant legal norms for ascertaining harm and liability are formalized in the law of property, torts, contracts, crimes, and such other bodies of law as antitrust and regulation. Property is thus imbedded in a larger normative framework, which cannot be discussed here.

EFFICIENCY OF A PURE PROPERTY REGIME

Property serves several purposes. First, it constitutes a significant aspect of liberty, a quality that is important for its own sake, independent of its effects. Second, property helps to preserve liberty by decentralizing power and resisting tyranny. Third, it promotes efficiency, which is the focus of this essay.

Ideally, the law pertaining to property internalizes the effects of using resources. *Internalization* means that all the benefits and costs of the owner's actions accrue to him, not to others. To achieve internalization, property law assigns to the owner the immediate benefits and costs from using a resource, but sometimes resource use causes spillovers, such as pollution of air, reduction of light, or contamination of water. Nuisance law assigns liability for spillovers to the owner of the resource that causes them. Similarly, risks are sometimes imposed on others by, say, driving cars, blasting rocks, serving food that can spoil, or selling potentially defective products. When these risks materialize, the law of torts may assign liability for the resulting harm to the owner of the resource that caused it.[2] The law of nuisance and torts can thus be viewed as a mechanism for internalizing costs.

Fairness requires that people who cause harm must compensate their victims, or so it seems to many lawyers. When internalization is perfect, so is compensation. What is more important for efficiency, however, is that perfect compensation causes all the costs and benefits from using property to enter into the decision calculus of a self-interested owner. Assigning the net benefits of resource use to its owner gives him an incentive to maximize them. Maximizing the net benefits from resource use requires enterprise and innovation, which makes the economy productive. So internalization is both fair and efficient.

Besides internalization, property law promotes efficiency by channeling transactions into voluntary exchange. Much of microeconomic theory since Adam Smith has been built on the insight that trade usually benefits everyone who engages in it, and competitive markets maximize the total surplus from trade. Property law promotes trade, in the first instance, by providing a clear and secure definition of ownership rights. To illustrate, a public registry of deeds assures the purchasers of real estate that their titles are clear. Conversely, obscure or insecure ownership rights burden an exchange with high information costs and heavy risk discounting.

These remarks about trade and law are succinctly summarized in the technical language of economics. Economists lump together information costs, risk discounting, and coordination costs into the general category of *transaction costs*. Thus one can say that ideally the law pertaining to property promotes trade by minimizing the transaction costs of exchange.

ORGANIZATION AS PROPERTY

The pure property regime just sketched has never been realized historically. The regulation of markets for corporate control is an inevitable part of contemporary capitalism, although regulation usually goes far beyond what efficiency requires. To explain why, I must analyze the ownership of organizations. Any organization can own property, as when a corporation owns real estate. In addition, some organizations can *be* property, as when Henry Ford owned the Ford Motor Company. Sole proprietorships, partnerships, and closely held corporations are pure property. Property in this sense is a *form* of organization. To be property, an organization must have a form that gives someone discretion over it. Discretion is conveyed by a full and complete set of rights, as listed above, including the right to use, improve, develop, transform, reorganize, deplete, destroy, sell, donate, bequeath, mortgage, or lease the organization.

Organizations that cannot be property can own it. Thus a cooperative or government can own property such as real estate, machinery, patents, and trademarks. The property of a cooperative or government can be sold, and the contractual rights can be assigned. But an organization is not its assets, just as a person is not the property that he or she owns. Cooperatives and governments cannot be sold because they are not themselves property.

To understand why some organizations can be property and others cannot, the general idea of an organization must be explained. From a sociological viewpoint, an organization is a structure of offices and roles capable of corporate action. An office is a job with legal powers and obligations explicitly attached to it. The fundamental offices in a business organization are usually defined and powers are allocated to them in a constitutional document such as a corporate charter. The organization's constitution also stipulates how to make operating rules.

Much of the activity of the organization follows informal practices, not formal rules laid down in its constitution or operating rules. The informal practices are organized around roles formed by shared expectations about the division of labor. To illustrate, the accountant's role includes keeping the books, and the secretary's role includes transcribing reports. The people who perform roles often have employment contracts, but the contracts do not explicitly state in detail what the employees' powers and duties are.

Offices and roles can be structured to direct people's efforts towards common goals, whose pursuit constitutes corporate action. To facilitate corporate action in a business organization, offices and roles are usually arranged hierarchically. Information flows up the hierarchy, and orders flow down it. Hierarchical structure gives the organization the capacity to act quickly and decisively. Some businesses have departed from the traditional hierarchical model and formed decentralized networks. Such a network remains a single organization so long as it retains the capacity for corporate action. If this capacity is lost, the network is best described as a relationship among different organizations.

Inside an organization, people have offices and roles that coordinate their behavior. Outside the organization, goods are exchanged in markets, and behavior is coordinated by prices. Thus the boundary of an organization is formed by the markets in which it operates. For example, the Ford Motor Company needs tires for its automobiles. Ford could either go outside its organization and buy tires on the market from another manufacturer, or it could establish a subsidiary to manufacture tires. Production in a subsidiary keeps the activity within the same organization.

When an organization is pure property, the owner has the legal right to choose its goals. In addition, the owner can restructure its offices and roles to suit his own ends. Thus the owner can transform, dissolve, merge, or sell the organization in whole or part. In a corporation or partnership, these ownership rights are conveyed by the organization's constitutional document and by applicable law. In a cooperative or government, which is not property, ownership rights are suppressed by the organization's constitution and applicable laws, which limit any individual's discretionary power over the organization.

As explained, property conveys discretion on the owner to do as he pleases with it. An alternative is to vest power in a group of people acting collectively. For instance, the members of a cooperative usually determine how to use its assets by majority vote. When several parties must participate in a decision, a problem of governance exists. Thus the alternative to property in organizations is politics. Property is a form of individual choice, whereas nonproperty control of resources is usually a form of collective choice.

The economic advantage of an organization having an owner is the same as for any other resource. Specifically, ownership aligns incentives for effort and risk-taking by internalizing the benefits and costs of resource use. The same person—the owner—determines the organization's structure and also enjoys the resulting profits, or suffers the resulting losses. In addition, only organizations that are property can be bought and sold. Trade in organizations, like trade in toothbrushes or oil wells, usually creates a surplus. Empirical research on the stock market indicates a substantial surplus from buying companies.[3] The surplus often arises from replacing inferior management, cutting unprofitable product lines, and rearranging industrial structure to take advantage of complementarities and synergies. The sale of an organization redeploys its resources very quickly, enabling rapid adjustment to changes in technology and demand.

Organizational property also has disadvantages. Concentrating benefits and costs in an individual focuses risk, whereas risk spreading may be more efficient. Also, the owner's discretion over the organization may undermine the loyalty of its members, as will be explained later. An advantage of governance over property concerns norms. An old tradition in Western thought, called contractarianism, holds that the law's authority comes from the consent of the people to whom it applies. Consent is more likely to result in voluntary or enthusiastic compliance than in evasion or grudging compliance. A system of governance in an organization may generate consent and create effective norms better than a system of ownership. So property and nonproperty forms of organization each have their advantages and disadvantages.

PROPERTY AS A FRAMEWORK FOR COMPETITION

Organizations compete for money and members. Ideally, those organizations should flourish that are judged best by the people who decide where to invest and what to join. The law should be neutral in this competition. To achieve neutrality, the law declares that organizations are "legal persons" and formulates property law in terms of the rights and obligations of people. An owner ideally has the same property rights over material resources whether that owner is an individual, family, clan, tribe, partner, stockholder, cooperative, corporation, collective, foundation, pension fund, bank, or government. Thus a pure property regime takes no interst in the identity of owners.

The indifference of law to an owner's identity helps to create a neutral legal framework. To understand why, contrast property that is actively traded, such as toothbrushes and trucks, with property that seldom changes owners, such as Rembrandt's paintings. If the market for organizations is active, they change owners from time to time, becoming the subsidiary first of one company and then another. In inactive markets, organizations persist for long periods as the property of the same legal person, such as a large holding company.

Active markets are needed for competition. An important question of public policy toward any market concerns the legal framework needed to sustain competition. In the most favorable circumstances, law sustains competition merely by defining and enforcing property rights. An industry is naturally competitive when the efficient scale of production is small relative to demand for the industry's product. In the absence of collusion, a naturally competitive industry is very active, and it has too many buyers and sellers for any one of them to influence prices. Alternatively, a natural monopoly exists when competition extinguishes itself because economies of scale are large relative to demand, so that the largest producer always has the lowest costs.

Unfortunately, a market for large organizations inevitably has at least two elements of natural monopoly. First, potential buyers may hesitate to purchase an organization unless they possess the technical knowledge required to manage it. To illustrate, the primary candidates to acquire a failing airline are other airlines, and there are few airlines in many markets. Second, potential buyers of large organizations are limited to those who can assemble sufficient capital, and capital markets are notoriously imperfect.

Policymakers often face a trade-off between monopoly power in markets for products and organizations. For example, if the antitrust authorities allow one airline to acquire another, competition decreases in the market for airline travel. If the antitrust authorities forbid one airline from acquiring another, competition decreases in the market for airline companies. Similarly, if the antitrust authorities allow small banks to merge or collaborate in order to finance the purchase of large companies, competition may decrease in the market for financial services. Conversely, if the banking industry is fragmented by law as in the United States, few buyers exist for large organizations.

BIASED FRAMEWORKS

The element of natural monopoly partly accounts for inactivity in markets for organizations, but contract and law are also important. To see why, recall that a pure property regime allows the owner to do anything with the resource that does not harm others. The constraint of not harming others becomes problematic when the property is an organization staffed by people. People in an organization, unlike a toothbrush or oil well, have legal and moral rights, and their interests and welfare are matters of public concern.

Restructuring an organization and retargeting its goals directly affects the welfare of its members. People care about the offices and roles assigned to them. They want good, secure jobs. To achieve job security, the current holders of jobs seek to limit the rights of the owners to restructure the organization. Ownership rights over organizations are typically circumscribed and regulated rather than full and complete.

The limits most familiar to the public concern the protection of workers. Less familiar, but no less important to productivity, are the protections for directors and managers. I cannot survey the variety of executive protections from one country to another, but I can mention a few examples. A vivid American example is the so-called golden parachute. This phrase refers to generous severance pay guaranteed to executives in the event that they lose their jobs in a hostile takeover of the company. The severance pay can be large enough to deter corporate raiders.

In Germany, corporate charters of large firms often contain a "5 percent rule," which stipulates that no single stockholder can have more than 5 percent of the votes even if he owns more than 5 percent of the stock. As a result of this rule, German banks enjoy secure control over many German companies, since owners leave stocks on deposit at the banks, and the banks have the right to vote them. Thus the banks, unlike other large investors, have more than 5 percent of the votes in the companies.[4] German banks almost never relinquish control over their client corporations.

In Japan, job security is more a matter of role than contract. The corporate culture favors employment for life, which includes managers. The main bank and the network of suppliers, which together own a controlling share of the corporation's stock, may shunt unsuccessful managers aside in the corporate hierarchy but will not fire them. Selling an organization is perceived as disloyal to its members.[5]

In these examples from three countries, limits on dismissing executives are imposed by contract or custom. These private agreements reduce the level of activity and competition in the market for organizations by increasing the cost and difficulty of restructuring and selling them. In addition to private agreements, limits on the market for organizations are usually imposed by law. To illustrate by an American example, the Williams Act requires someone who purchases 5 percent of the stock of a company to announce that fact publicly and to delay further purchases for a specified period of time.

Adam Smith observed that, monopoly being more profitable than competition, businessmen can seldom talk together without conspiring against the public. Are the agreements and laws protecting executives conspiracies against the public? This question has no simple answer. A golden parachute, for example, can be legitimate severance pay that enables a company to hire the most able managers, or it can be an insidious device for protecting inferior managers from competition. In spite of this complexity, a simple fact provides some guidance to law and policy. Executives are not a class of people who need the state's paternalistic protection. They have the knowledge and power to negotiate protection for themselves by private agreement. A strong argument thus exists against any laws or regulations ostensibly protecting executives or otherwise impeding the market for organizations on behalf of executives. Executive protection should arise from private agreement, never from law.

A more difficult question concerns whether law should refuse to enforce, or actively suppress, private agreements to protect executives. Should such agreements be suppressed by antitrust law on the ground that they are conspiracies to restrain trade? The question is complicated because private constraints in markets for organizations can promote efficiency if security induces loyalty and effort.

SEPARATION OF PROFITS AND POWER

When an organization is pure property, someone ideally possesses full discretion over it and also internalizes the net benefits of its use. To illustrate, power and responsibility are joined in a family business when the sole proprietor makes the decisions and absorbs the profits or losses. In modern capitalism, however, it is uneconomic for the owners of flourishing businesses to finance expansion internally. Funds must shift rapidly from one large organization to another in response to the market's creative destruction. To acquire funds quickly, corporations must sell bonds or stocks. A corporation that sells stock to the public is not wholly the property of the people who run it. In public corporations, sale of stock to the general public fragments and distributes the bundle of rights constituting ownership.

To understand fragmentation, consider the public corporation's governance. The stockholders are usually entitled to one vote per stock on matters of central importance to the corporation, including the choice of its directors. The directors in turn appoint management and approve policies. In closely held companies, a single person or small group of associates owns enough stock to control the election of directors. Secure control of small companies requires owning 51 percent of the shares. Control may be achieved in large companies by owning a much smaller percent.

Collective-choice theorists sometimes define the "power" of a vote as the probability that it will be decisive. For instance, each vote is powerful in a close election between two candidates, and each vote has little power in a landslide victory by one candidate. The power of a vote belonging to the controlling block of a company is high, whereas the power of a vote by a minority shareholder is nil. Controlling shareholders hold power and enjoy part of the profits. Minority shareholders enjoy part of the profits and hold no power.

In reality, the managers of a corporation often control it even though they own a small percent of its stock. Thus power and responsibility are imperfectly conjoined in a public corporation. The resulting separation of profits and power, which is called the separation of ownership from control, has been studied intensively, most recently by game theorists.[6] In the standard formulation, the stockholders are described as the "principal" and management is described as an "agent." The principal-agent problem is to design an incentive scheme in which that agent's best interest is served by doing what benefits the principal the most.

A perfect solution to the principal-agent problem is an incentive scheme such that the agent maximizes his own utility or income when his actions maximize the principal's utility or income. A perfect solution typically requires the principal's information about the agent's behavior to be perfect. In reality, the principal's information is highly imperfect, so the agent usually has incentives to do some acts that benefit him at the principal's expense. Thus the principal-agent problem raised by the modern corporation does not have a perfect solution.

In this imperfect world, a variety of means are employed by contract and law to elicit effort and appropriate risk-taking from managers.

Contractual solutions include stock options to increase management's share of ownership, and bonuses or performance pay to reward effort and results. Legal solutions include civil and criminal liability, especially for breach of fiduciary duty. Fiduciary law is noteworthy for its clean solution to the problem of asymmetrical information. Stockholders seldom obtain sufficient evidence of manager's wrongdoing to satisfy the standards of proof ordinarily demanded by courts. Consequently, fiduciary law departs from the usual requirement of proof and presumes wrongdoing from its appearance. For example, a manager who appropriates a corporate opportunity is presumed by law to have damaged the stockholders, and he must disgorge the profits to the corporation even if damage to the stockholders cannot be proved.[7]

A familiar fact of business life is that people are more inclined toward sharp practices or cheating in short-run relationships than in long-run relationships. The corresponding technical proposition is that many inefficiencies in one-shot games disappear in repeated games.[8] Consequently, lengthening the time horizon helps solve the principal-agent problem. The time horizon is lengthened by contracts and practices that create job security and loyalty among executives. The optimal solutions to the principal-agent problem often rely on contracts and practices that sustain long-run relationships.

Creating monopoly power for members of an organization builds loyalty to it. Who would quit a job that pays monopoly wages to take a job that pays competitive wages? Lawmakers and regulators thus face the need to devise optimal solutions to the principal-agent problem and to control private agreements to create monopoly profits for executives. I offer no general solution for this problem because it has none. It has no general solution because the relevant markets are naturally too thin to be perfectly competitive.

Scholars sometimes say that only four numbers should matter to antitrust policy: one, two, three,and four-or-more. This cryptic phrase means that a market with four or more suppliers behaves much like a perfectly competitive market, whereas each reduction in suppliers below four increases the likelihood of monopolistic practices. Although not strictly true, this rule of thumb provides a focal point for discussing markets for organizations.

For purposes of discussion, ignore complexities like import competition, contestable markets, and barriers to entry. Assume that when the market for organizations has, say, four or more active participants, it is naturally large enough for effective competition. Assume, for example, that more than four airlines compete against one another. Furthermore, assume that they actively search for airline companies to acquire and that no airlines companies have created obstacles to hostile takeovers. By assumption, the market for airline organizations is naturally competitive. Now suppose that a contract between an airline and its executives creates obstacles to a takeover, such as golden parachutes. By assumption, the golden parachutes remove this company from the market for takeovers.

The antitrust authorities must decide whether to allow its removal. The preceding rule of thumb suggests an answer. If at least four companies remain in the market, the market will probably remain competitive. Consequently, the antitrust authorities should allow the restrictive contract. In general, private restrictions that inhibit competition for owning organizations are not troublesome if they effectively remove one company from a market with more than four competitors. Under such conditions of workable competition, the law can provide a neutral framework for competition among organizations and thus realize the ideal of a pure property regime. Competition will subsequently determine whether the restrictive contract is inferior or superior to unrestricted contracts.

To illustrate, suppose the law permitted organizations to make contracts with executives that interfere with takeovers or restructuring. Some manufacturers might form tight links with banks, as in Germany; others might form networks with a main bank and suppliers, as in Japan; still others might maintain distance from banks and networks, as in America. If enough companies of different types exist, competition among them will decide in time which form of organization is more efficient.

This scenario assumes a large market for corporate control so that diverse types of organizations can coexist. To consider the opposite possibility, return to the example of the airline company that wants to preclude hostile takeovers. However, change the assumptions and assume that *fewer* than four companies remain in the market for corporate control after one company adopts restrictive practices to preclude a hostile takeover. The four-firm rule of thumb for antitrust law suggests that the market will become uncompetitive. Here the authorities face a tougher decision; prohibiting the contract may undermine the loyalty to firms that is needed to solve the principal-agent problem.

This dilemma has no general policy solution. When the market for organizations is thin, a neutral framework is impossible. Instead, the law must adopt a policy of enforcing or suppressing the relevant contracts and practices.

Unfortunately neither theory nor empirical research provides clear guidance to lawmakers. The differences between the American, German, and Japanese systems have been inadequately analyzed and researched in spite of intensive policy debate. At this point, scholars can only guess about the best policy. My guess is that companies should be private or public depending on their stage in the industry's history. Failing companies that must be restructured need the decisiveness and agility of private owners, whereas companies that are flourishing and expanding need access to public funds. So my guess is that the best legal framework would permit transitions from public to private organization, and back again. These remarks, however, only hint at the issues involved in a complex subject.[9]

PROPERTY THEORY APPLIED TO RUSSIA

The communist revolutions in Europe went beyond regulating private property and attempted to abolish it. Not all forms of private property were abolished, but private property as a form of organization in large enterprises was eliminated in all communist countries. Property theory offers an interpretation of the consequences, which I outline briefly. The aim of state socialism under Stalin was for the dictator to have complete discretion over economic life, including organizational structure, offices, roles, personnel, and material resources. If ownership is equated with discretion over resources, then Stalin owned everything. Stalinism was a period of pure monopoly.

His control was exercised through centralized planning, which proceeds by issuing commands backed by threats. The economic theory of deterrence offers an insight into the rationality of central planning under Stalin. A perfectly rational, self-interested person will disobey a command when the benefit of disobedience exceeds the expected sanction.[10] The expected sanction equals the magnitude of punishment times its probability. Raising the probability of punishing wrongdoing requires more police, more courts, more prosecutors, and so forth, which is costly. The cost is especially high for economic crimes, since catching offenders is difficult. In contrast, a bullet in the head is cheap. Similarly, the state can actually make a profit by enslaving the wrongdoer. Thus the efficient deterrence of many economic crimes calls for extremely harsh punishments, like shooting or enslaving people, applied with low probability and little discernment.[11] Deterrence theory implies that terror minimizes the costs of enforcing central planning. Stalin apparently enforced the central plan at moderate cost to government and at appalling human costs.

The Stalinist model of central planning enforced by terror was implemented in varying degrees by sector and country. Stalin's death created room for contending factions and more humane policies. Property theory explains how the growth of factions and the decline of terror may have contributed to falling economic growth rates in eastern Europe in the 1970s, which turned to stagnation in the 1980s.

As explained, terror is the rational way to enforce central planning. Once terror was abandoned, central planning became too costly to enforce, and the central plan lost its effectiveness. When the single dictator gave way to contending factions, no one had discretion over the entire economy. It was not owned by anyone; instead, property rights were diffuse. In socially owned enterprises, no one person or small group of people joined power and profit. Politics replaced discretion, collective choice replaced individual choice, and governance replaced commands.

Socially owned enterprises had different types of governance that varied by time and place, according to political currents.[12] A Hungarian scholar has argued that political ends were served by keeping ownership rights vague and uncertain in Hungarian enterprises. They were, in his view, owned by no one.[13] His findings remind me of a saying I heard in Croatia: "We know what social ownership isn't, but not what it is."

When property rights are diffuse and uncertain, people devote their energies to trying to secure property rather than to produce it. In general, game theory shows that uncertainty over entitlements diverts energies from production to redistribution. This result can be explained by analogy. When oil wells were first drilled in America, the party that pumped oil to the surface was entitled to keep it by law. In other words, oil in the ground was unowned, and oil raised to the surface was owned by the party that possessed it. As a consequence, oil companies raced each other to extract as much oil from the ground as quickly as possible. Oil in the ground is analogous to social property in the sense that no one clearly owns it. Consequently, people in post-communist countries are engaged in a wasteful race to remove property from social ownership and obtain private possession of it.

The race to appropriate social property is one cause of the spontaneous disintegration of socialist enterprises. After 1989, however, disintegration accelerated into a collapse in many countries. Game theory suggests why. When the legal framework for contract law is underdeveloped, so that promises are difficult to enforce, long-run relationships will replace contracts as a device for coordinating behavior.[14] Exchange in long-run relationships takes the form of reciprocal favors that follow the principle of "tit for tat" or "I'll scratch your back if you scratch mine." For example, a mechanic repairs a truck for the driver as a "favor," but the mechanic later receives a crate of oranges off the truck as a "gift." Economic agents engage in barter and keep implicit accounts to make sure they receive as much as they get.

State socialism thus replaced market exchange but with less efficient long-term reciprocal and political relationships. A problem arises with a system of reciprocity when the parties see it coming to an end. As the end draws near, economic agents begin to doubt that they will ever be paid back for the favors they do. Consequently, they are no longer willing to extend favors to others. A loss of faith in the future of social ownership thus undermines the reciprocal relationships that made it work. In technical terms, games have cooperative solutions when they are repeated indefinitely, whereas cooperation collapses when the game approaches its end (the "endgame problem").

WHICH CAPITALISM?

Russia has now entered a new era of privatization. Russian leaders perceive privatization as the only way out of their current dilemma. Because I cannot discuss all the aspects of privatization here, I will focus on organizational property. Many people in the post-communist countries observed that social ownership caused irresponsible management. They concluded, mistakenly, that a stock market will automatically cure the problem. Their mistake arises from their failure to distinguish between buying stock and buying a company. As explained, managers of capitalist corporations have devices for insulating themselves from outside pressures so that they can pursue ineffective or irresponsible policies. When a company has an owner with a controlling interest, that person or organization can force managers to be responsible, whereas dispersed stockholders cannot.

Germany, Japan, and the United States offer different models for overseeing managers. As explained, the controlling stockholders in Germany are banks; in Japan, the controlling stockholders are the company's main bank and suppliers; in the United States, most financial institutions like commercial banks are not allowed to own a controlling share of stocks. Instead, the United States has developed the practice of hostile takeovers, so that the market oversees the managers. The post-communist countries therefore face the question, which capitalism?

There can be no neutral framweork for competition to decide this question. Instead, it must be answered by law and policy. A neutral framework is impossible because the potential market for corporate control is not large enough for the full range of alternative forms of finance and control to compete with one another. When privatizing, the roles must be delineated for commercial banks, investment banks, mutual funds, insurance companies, and pension funds. Institutional investors are unlikely to relinquish any control that they exercise over the boards of directors during the privatization process. So the path taken in the transition to capitalism will probably have a decisive influence on the final result.

The current economic crisis in the post-communist countries demands a political solution. The privatization agencies will inevitably respond to politics. For example, in Croatia the privatization fund's director is appointed by the president of the Republic, and the fund will have access to tax revenues supplied by the state. The intimate connection between politics and finance creates many possibilities for political favoritism and corruption in the allocation of investment funds. Uncertainty about property rights multiplies the opportunities for political redistributions of wealth and undermines the confidence of investors.

In the long run, the government privatization funds must be liquidated or transformed into investment banks that are insulated from politics and operate on commercial principles. In the meantime, the course of privatization will be evolutionary in part and planned in part. The emphasis and direction of privatization will shift as political currents reverse themselves, voters gain more experience with capitalism, new issues become salient, and public priorities change. Space does not permit me to develop an economic analysis of legislation here, but such an analysis prompts pessimism about the likelihood of privatization leading to anything resembling a pure property regime.

SUMMARY AND CONCLUSION

Private property is a bundle of rights that gives owners discretion over the use of resources. Discretion implies that the owners are not answerable to other people or the state. This zone of privacy is an aspect of freedom and a bulwark against tyranny. In addition, private property creates incentives for efficiency and innovation. A pure property regime promotes efficiency by internalizing the costs and benefits of resource use, lubricating trade, and promoting efficient organization.

Some organizations can be an individual's property; others preclude individual ownership by their nature. Discretion and individual choice are aspects of organization property, whereas politics and collective choice are aspects of most nonproperty organizations. The Russian economy passed from monopoly ownership by Stalin to social ownership by political coalitions, and has now entered the era of privatization.

Private property and capitalism are not sufficient conditions to determine the form of corporate organization. Rather than prescribing a particular form, private property and capitalism ideally provide a framework for competition among alternative forms. In practice this framework cannot be perfectly neutral, because markets for organizations are thin rather than naturally competitive. To privatize is to depoliticize, but this process cannot go all the way. Russia must adopt financial institutions through laws that favor particular ways of choosing business leaders. Germany, Japan, and the United States provide alternative models.

Economic analysis of the legislative process provokes skepticism that privatization will lead to anything like a pure property regime. Legislation is directed toward efficiency in fits and starts as government responds to shifting political currents. Protection of property from political redistributions, which undermine the confidence of investors, requires a strong, independent judiciary.

Constitutional historians of the United States have identified certain moments in history when politicians and the public have been able to rise above immediate self-interest and respond to a larger vision.[15] In effect, these theories postulate behavior outside the economic model of self-interest, which leads to the creation of a constitutional framework for capitalism and democracy. The brightest hope for privatization in eastern Europe is that those countries will enjoy such a moment in their history right now.

NOTES

1. The relationship between property and liberty is an old theme in political philosophy. A thorough bibliography and critical discussion is in Laura S. Underkuffler, "On Property: An Essay," *Yale Law Journal*, vol. 100 (1990), pp. 127–48.

2. Causing harm is almost always necessary for liability. (Vicarious liability is the exception.) If causing harm is sufficient for liability, the rule of law is said to be "strict liability." In contrast, liability under a negligence rule requires the injurer to cause harm and also to be at fault.

3. The acquiring firm usually pays a premium and the higher stock price persists after the acquisition, while the acquiring firm's stock price remains largely unchanged. See Jensen and Ruback, "The Market for Corporate Control: The Scientific Evidence," *Journal of Financial Economics*, vol. 11 (1983), pp. 5–50.

4. See Theodor Baums, "Banks and Corporate Control," John M. Olin Working Papers in Law and Economics 90-1 (University of California at Berkeley, School of Law, 1991).

5. See Zenichi Shishido, "Comparative Business Systems: US-Japan" (two lectures), University of California at Berkeley, School of Law, 1991.

6. See the principal-agent literature, such as B. R. Holmstrom and J. Tirole, "Theory of the Firm," in R. Schmalensee and R. Willig, *Handbook of Industrial Organization* (Amsterdam: North-Holland, 1989); and Jean Tirole, *The Theory of Industrial Organization* (MIT Press, 1988).

7. See Robert Cooter and Bradley J. Freedman, "The Fiduciary Relationship: Its Economic Character and Legal Consequences," *New York University Law Review*, vol. 66 (October 1991), pp. 1045–75.

8. In general, see Drew Fudenberg and Eric Maskin, "The Folk Theorem in Repeated Games with Discounting or with Incomplete Information," *Econometrica*, vol. 54 (1986), pp. 533–54. For application to the law of contracts, see

Gillian K. Hadfield, "Problematic Relations: Franchising and the Law of Incomplete Contracts," *Stanford Law Review*, vol. 42 (1990), pp. 927–92.

9. For example, my analysis commends leveraged buy-outs by which management takes a failing company private, yet these transactions have been called the "ultimate insider trading."

10. I assume risk neutrality of the agent.

11. See Gary Becker, "Crime and Punishment: An Economic Approach," *Journal of Political Economy*, vol. 76 (1968), pp. 169–217.

12. Mancur Olsen is responsible for this theory.

13. See A. Sajo, "Diffuse Rights in Search of an Agent: A Property Rights Analysis of the Firm in the Socialist Market Economy," *International Review of Law and Economics*, vol. 10 (1990), pp. 41–60.

14. See Robert Cooter with Janet Landa, "Personal v. Impersonal Trade and the Optimal Size of Clubs," *International Review of Law and Economics*, vol. 4 (1984), pp. 15–22; and Robert Cooter, "Inventing Market Property: The Land Court of Papua New Guinea," *Law and Society Review*, vol. 25 (1991), pp. 759–802.

15. Bruce A. Ackerman, "The Storrs Lectures: Discovering the Constitution," *Yale Law Journal*, vol. 93 (1984), pp. 1013–72.

Fertile Money

It was Aristotle who said that money is sterile, meaning unproductive or without yield. This isn't always strictly so. But it has been near enough the truth throughout history to deserve explanation. The apparent reason is that the qualities we want in money seldom appear in high-yield assets, but they have paid for themselves by saving us the transaction costs of barter.

Money evolved as a measure of value and a medium of exchange. It should be something actually wanted, and steadily so over time. It should also be something "liquid," meaning fungible, plentiful, divisible, storable, and transportable. *Fungible* here means homogeneous or interchangeable, like peas in a pod.

Merchants found long ago that gold and silver can have those qualities. Precious metals are desired, if for elusive reasons, and so much so that small weights carry high purchasing power. This makes them easy to store and transport. If they are of even purity, they are fungible and divisible. They are also "noble," or chemically difficult to synthesize or degrade. This quality guards against counterfeiting and lowers maintenance costs. Gold and silver, however, are classically sterile apart from their output of "psychic rewards" to owners. Many today prefer other psychic rewards and more fruitful assets. The value of those metals, moreover, depends on supply, which may change unexpectedly with new discoveries or with the policies of foreign governments that control them.

AN ANALYSIS OF MONEY IN THE MODERN WORLD

Precious metals and other commodities will have a place in my scenario for the future evolution of money. Meanwhile I will first consider money in the modern world.

Most money transactions today are settled with currency or with transfers between bank accounts. Thus money is essentially currency plus deposits. Most value and transaction volume is carried by the latter.

Commercial banks are highly leveraged "debt intermediaries." Defying Polonius, they are both borrowers and lenders. They borrow from depositors to relend to clients at a higher rate. Stockholders pocket the difference after expenses. Leverage is high because deposits owed back to depositors have typically run some five to twenty times stockholders' equity. Assuming for the moment that the system works or can be made to work, how does money come into existence, and what happens to it?

When a bank lends money against a client's promissory note, it usually effects the loan by setting up an account for the client which he can draw down as he likes. This account is not transferred from other deposits or from cash. It is simply created. And since deposits are money, this new one adds to the money supply. But because the bank also has the new promissory note to offset it, there is as much added wealth in the bank as added claims against it in the form of deposits. The increase is not of itself money destabilizing.

The Federal Reserve Bank creates currency in much the same way. When it lends to member banks or government by "rediscounting" promissory notes or buying government bonds, it too effects these loans by setting up accounts. These can be withdrawn in Federal Reserve notes, meaning the greenbacks in our wallets. The Fed simply prints these greenbacks, but it prints them against notes and bonds received. Currency, like deposit money, grows in equal measure to assets on hand, and the growth need not be inflationary.

But neither does this initial balance inhibit inflation once money is created, as will be seen. Meanwhile one can say that money in the modern world, apart from coins, is created in banks. Except for pocket currency, it is also largely stored in them and has been for some three centuries. For these reasons, one can reasonably speak of modern money as "bank money."

Collateral and Backing

The words *collateral* and *backing* are sometimes used interchangeably, but they can be distinguished.

Collateral is something pledged to a lender in case of default. It helps assure him that the number of dollars lent will be recovered, but not that they will keep their purchasing power. This is true because any collateral value under default will presumably go to residual claimants after lenders are paid off. Thus a ten-dollar IOU collateralized by a diamond as big as the Ritz is still worth no more than ten dollars.

Backing of money means something different. While collateral adds confidence that dollars lent will be returned, backing adds confidence that a dollar will hold its value over time. For example, currency units in some countries can be exchanged at banks for specified weights of gold or silver so long as supplies of these hold out. That was true in the United States until about twenty years ago. Gold and silver coins meanwhile can be called self-backing insofar as their weight is worth their nominal value.

One sufficient test of backing, though perhaps not a necessary one, is utility or market value independent of purchasing power. Money is backed if people want it as much to keep as to spend, or is convertible into such a thing. Could a debt instrument count as backing by this test? Not really. It is true that a spendable bond would be wanted independently for yield. Yet the real value or utility of the yield would vary as the value of the money yielded. Desire for a spendable bond would be independent of the owner's purchasing or income-earning intent, but not of the bond's purchasing power. And as just mentioned, this must be as ture of a collateralized bond as an uncollateralized one.

Sometimes there are proposals to make money redeemable in debt instruments. I refer to this technique as soft backing. Hard backing, or simply backing, means commodity or other equity interests tending to hold constant in real rather than nominal value.

One can say that bank money in this country is efffectively collateralized as it is created but that it is unbacked. The collateral protecting moneyholders consists of the promissory notes and bonds from clients and government which commercial banks and the Federal Reserve Bank have in hand as they create deposits or banknotes against them. These assets help enable banks to repay moneyholders, but they are not backing because they do nothing to ensure the purchasing power of the dollars repaid.

If collateral value varies with market value, it can give a faithful picture of the worth of money at the moment collateral is given. But it can do nothing to influence that worth. Collateral is a time-specific *measure* of money value, while backing is a cause of value.

Risk Aversion and Equilibrium Debt Ratio

An important question is why some people prefer to be debtors and others to be creditors. Experience suggests that equities or residual interests yield more than fixed-income securities. A common and likely explanation is that equity receives a premium for risk. How does this work?

My first assumption is that real incomes from unencumbered investments are not perfectly steady. Risk-averse investors can be loosely defined as those who prefer more steadiness than the average for investments at the same average income expectation. Risk preferrers like less steadiness, and the remaining investors are risk neutral. The second assumption is that more wealth is in the hands of risk-averse investors than of equally risk-preferring ones. The risk averse favor the seniority and steadiness of bonds (if they trust that any inflation risk is discounted in interest rates). But arithmetic shows that fixed obligations, or leverage, in an imperfectly steady world must make residual income to equity holders even more volatile than before. Since risk-averse or bond-favoring investors cannot find enough risk-preferring or risk-neutral ones to allow a trade of stocks for bonds of equal profit expectation, they must concede more profit for more steadiness. Bargaining between them leads to an equilibrium debt ratio.

But intentions do not always govern outcomes. Debt is more immune to business risks, and equity to inflation or deflation risks. Bonds and their real yields must indeed be steadier when inflation is absent or exactly predictable. In this century it has been neither, and it is difficult at best to make bank money stable. The relative real-dollar stability of equities versus loans of a given maturity should be settled by observation rather than by reasoning a priori.

Bank Structure

Banks lend money at interest rates dictated by the market. But, as mentioned, these rates are lower than the rates of return needed to attract stockholders. Consequently, bank stockholders must somehow parlay a lower yield into a higher one even while paying expenses.

Like other financial institutions, they do so by devices called spread and leverage.

To simplify things, suppose that a bank's assets are made up of loans receivable and nothing else. The right side of its balance sheet includes only deposits and stockholders' equity. *Leverage* is defined as loans divided by stockholders' equity, and *expense ratio* as loans divided by expense rate. Expenses include income tax but exclude interest paid to depositors. Interest rate received from borrowers less expense ratio is called *operating margin*; this, less interest rate paid to depositors, is called *spread*.

The rate of return to stockholders after tax is

$$(operating\ margin) + [(leverage) \times (spread)].$$

What does this mean? As noted, deposits are withdrawable on demand or are generally short term. Otherwise they could hardly serve as money. If the bank lends for much longer terms, the result is maturity mismatch, or misintermediation. This risks illiquidity if deposits shrink. As a result, it destabilizes banks and requires a higher rate of return to stockholders. Short maturities, on the other hand, imply low risk to lenders and so carry low interest rates. These mean a low operating margin and spread. That puts upward pressure on leverage in order to arrive at a market return, and so destabilizes banks once again.

Banks in fact carry much higher leverage than other businesses and have been shaky investments since their invention some three centuries ago. Leverage would disappear if banks turned their depositors into stockholders and depositor interest into dividends.

The Layered Money Supply

As mentioned, bank money is currency plus deposits. These are not identical in their "moneyness"; moreover, some deposits are more moneylike than others. Economists recognize several kinds of money and near-money. But how do they fit the qualities that money ought to have?

Is bank money fungible? Currency is, but deposits differ in interest and terms from bank to bank and from one type of deposit to another. Banks also differ in safety. Accounts are insured up to $100,000 only, and even within this limit insurance may not save depositors from all nuisance costs when new banking relationships must be built. Deposit money, then, can be called reasonably fungible.

Currency and deposits score well on the other liquidity tests of money. They are ample in supply, and sometimes too much so. Currency is easily stored and carried, and deposits can be shifted at electronic speeds and volumes. Both are also divisible with the qualification that large purchases may call for checks and small ones for currency. Currency tends to be the most widely accepted form of money and can be passed from hand to hand with no need for check-clearing expenses. That is why it usually offers low transaction costs when purchases are small.

Next come checkable deposits. These are less sure to be accepted in payment, since sellers may not trust buyers or banks or credit cards they don't know. Such deposits often minimize transaction costs where they are accepted and where purchases are large enough. These deposits plus currency and traveler's checks add up to what economists call transaction money, or M1.

M2 is M1 plus what is sometimes called near-money—mainly savings deposits, time deposits under $100,000, and money market funds in banks and outside them. These matter to the money supply because they can be converted into transaction money reasonably soon. Larger measures of money also exist, but do not need to be reviewed here.

Holding Costs

What does it cost to own money? I define the holding cost, or opportunity cost, of money as the added income other investments of comparable stability might have provided if money was held and not spent. Thus holding cost is income missed. Offsetting it is what might be called the transaction advantage of money, because of its greater convenience than barter for trading. Since some purchases will be more urgent or advantageous than others, and harder to effect without money, one expects money ownership to show diminishing returns to scale. One expects people to prefer to own just enought money for marginal transaction advantage and marginal holding cost to cancel out. The ratio of this money supply to national wealth can be called the efficiency point.

Does money in fact impose a holding cost? Currency in its present form yields nothing. Interest on checkable accounts varies, as noted earlier, but it is usually well below Treasury bill rates. Still, there is some room for doubt. It costs banks something to process checks, and these costs are often underbilled to the depositor. In effect, checking is subsidized by an artifically low deposit-interest yield. When allowance is made for this subsidy, it is harder to prove that money on the whole carries a holding cost. But this argument will not require an assumption that it does. I assert only that the holding cost offsets the transaction advantage *at* the *efficiency point*, and exceeds it in further increments of the money supply.

Monetary Techniques

Banks and governments try to control the supply of unbacked money for want of any other way to maintain its value. The devices they use are summed up as monetary policy. Its basic assumption and rationale is that the ratio of outlays on new goods and services to money supply is reasonably constant, at least over the time scale needed to bring monetary tactics to bear. This ratio is sometimes called the income velocity. If it were not reasonably steady, then one money supply might be scarcely more inflationary than another.

Is it steady in fact? If money imposes a holding cost, one expects it to be owned sparingly and for spending only. Competition to make do with less of it should help hold the velocity of money, or ratio of total purchases to money supply, somewhere near its practical maximum. Then is this maximum constant? That depends on circumstances. In unsettled times, the need for outlays might become lumpier without a change in the overall spending rate. More money on hand would be needed, and its velocity would drop.

Likewise an economic downturn might make people resort to older goods and so enlarge the second-hand market. The issue here for monetary purposes is double counting. More reselling means more money spent even when prices hold constant. That is why monetary policy assumes a steady income velocity as distinct from a steady velocity of money.

Under this assumption a money supply exists that is neither inflationary nor deflationary. The ratio of this supply to total wealth can be called the stability point. Where then does it lie at a given moment? Logic suggests that planners must gauge both current income and current money supply and know the stable ratio between them. In fact, none of the three proves easy to pin down. This problem has led economic theory to find ingenious shortcuts. Monetarists, for example, would simply expand the money supply at the long-term real growth rate. Others favor the golden rule of commodity tracking. These analysts reason that many actively traded commodities, including minerals and perishables alike, are largely uniform both physically and in human utility from one year to the next. If so, a general change in their current trading prices could give an up-to-the-minute reading of money instability. Planners then need only drop the money supply with each price uptick of a hypothetical "commodity basket," and conversely.

Both these shortcuts simplify measurement. The real growth rate can be predicted within tolerable error, and the current price for a given commodity mix is known exactly. But, as shown, the money supply may be defined in various ways. Meanwhile some critics find the monetarist regime too procrustean, and the commodity guideline too narrowly based. The fact that economists do not closely agree on monetary targets is instructive.

How do economists try to hit these targets? Given time, the central bank can raise or lower deposits by an opposite change in the required reserve ratio or in the rediscount rate it charges member banks. This last technique pushes their interest rates in the same direction. Higher interest means less demand for the new loans against which money is created, and lower interest does the opposite. But it is hard to say just how much money, and when, will be added or taken away by a given rate change.

Open-market techniques are faster if less enduring. Typically, government or the central bank might sell government bonds to moneyholders and so dry up some of the money supply. Buying bonds back puts new money into their hands. In this case it is hard to foresee how much of a new bond issue will be bought by the public rather than by banks, or how much will be sold by each into a tender.

Double Criticality

Here I assume nonetheless that the stability point can be identified, and this money target hit. But, as noted, there is also an efficiency point at which moneyholding cost balances the transaction cost of barter. Just as any departure from the former means money instability, any departure from the latter means more cost and so less output. That is to say, any departure from the latter is to some extent recessionary.

But inflation and deflation mean less real output too. That is why money stability is desirable. Like stable weights and measures, stable money simplifies description. It makes contracts easier to interpret and administer, and their outcomes easier to predict. Instability either up or down means poorer foresight and costlier exchanges. Though too little money is probably more dangerous than too much, both reduce real output.

Output is then maximized by hitting both balancing points. But do these optima agree? I for one can't think of a reason to believe either that they tend to do so or that they don't. Lack of such a reason should add to doubts about the practicality of strategies to stabilize unbacked money by controlling its supply.

Debt Neutrality

One can define equity or residual interest as the market value of any economic good less debt against it. Thus Exxon or a share of Exxon or a can of oil or an oil comodity future, less encumbrance, are all equity. Debt against it may be positive or zero. An equity is "debt neutral" when debt owed equals debt receivable in observed or inferred market value.

I said earlier that equity makes good backing because it is more or less inflation proof. Why? Inflation can be defined as a rise in the price of equivalent consumer goods or the means of producing them. Equity interests in this broad sense *are* these goods, loosely speaking, and are therefore the measure of price stability.

Which equities do I mean? Minerals? Land? Buildings? They might include all these and more. Ongoing businesses retain value, even as their component assets wear out and are replaced, because they compete to maximize it in a world of finite opportunity. The potential backing for money can be the universe of actively traded residual rights.

But that is not enough. Although unencumbered equities may be inflation proof, many equities in fact carry debt against them. Since the market value of debt tends to shrink when inflation is more than the amount discounted in interest rates, encumbered equities do the opposite: they end up owing cheaper dollars than they expected to owe. They should rise in real as well as nominal value under unforeseen inflation, and conversely, when things are equal. Only debt-neutral equities, including unencumbered ones, can expect to hold constant in real value when prices fluctuate. The reason is that debt owing to them and debt owed by them must vary alike. In this sense they are inflation immune.

It is true that equity interests owing debt at inflation-indexed rates may also be immune. But the question is how to get rid of inflation rather than how to live with it. Debt-neutral equities can provide the backing that makes this possible.

To put the case for debt-neutrality in more intuitive terms: If money or its backing is a right to a money income stream or is encumbered by money debt, to that extent its definition is circular. Only when these rights and burdens cancel can one say clearly what it is.

Debt-Neutral Mutual Funds

An investor might own 1 percent of a corporation that owes a net debt of one million dollars. Roughly speaking, he can debt-neutralize his investment by also buying ten thousand dollars worth of bonds. Ideally he should buy bonds identical to those against the corporation. In this way he might hope to cancel debt effects exactly on the value of his shares. A more practical answer might be to appraise the current market value of the company's debt rather than its face or book amount, and then buy reasonably similar bonds of 1 percent of that value. Here the investor would trust the market to maintain proportionate values at 1 percent thereafter.

A mutual fund might mix debt and equities by this formula and so maintain debt neutrality. Debt-neutral funds, I will argue, can become a source of self-backed money and a means of backing other money as well.

Fund Money

Ownership rights in nonbank mutual funds are usually held in units traded in securities markets. Like other publicly traded rights, they have certain moneylike qualities. They are actually desired. They are fungible in that one unit is interchangeable with another within a given fund. They are plentiful enough to make active trading practical. They are divisible to the extent that the individual unit is priced low. They are stored and tranported electronically at arbitrary volumes and distances. If improved further in the first three qualities, they might serve as money.

How might they be improved? As pointed out, funds can be made more stable if debt-neutralized. Units of a given value would become more plentiful if funds grew larger in aggregate. Funds could grow by issuing new units and buying equities and bonds with the proceeds. A single debt-neutral fund might grow until its size exceeded the transaction money supply of the economy. It might issue just enough units, through splits or reverse splits, to set the value of each at one current dollar. It could then maintain this value by continuous control either of fund size or of number of units outstanding. Units might then meet all the liquidity qualities while also holding a market value independent of purchasing power. That makes them what I have called self-backing.

A single fund so large might mean too little competition. That could prove impractical or impolitic. In this case a number of independent funds could serve if each maintained unit price at one dollar. One can speak of any money so derived as fund money.

Unit Price Pegging

Many corporations perform occasional stock splits and reverse splits in order to keep stock prices within familiar ranges. After each such change a stockholder has more or fewer shares of different individual value but the same aggregate value. He neither gains nor loses. In a computer age, it is possible to realign prices automatically with every transaction reported in the market. With every tick of the tape, a stockholder might have a fractionally different number of shares of a different value each.

A corporation or mutual fund following this policy might be said to issue dollar-pegged shares or units if these securities were maintained in value at one dollar. Pegging would work by free market action. Thus if a transaction took place at $1.01, a computer program would instantly raise share number or unit number in proportion, and conversely. The formula fed into the computer would be

$$\frac{new\ number\ of\ shares}{last\ number\ of\ shares} = \frac{last\ market\ transaction}{one\ dollar}$$

and each stockholder's account would adjust automatically in number. Thus buyers and sellers might agree at any price, presumably near a dollar, and prices would readjust to one dollar immediately after.

In practice, so automatic a pegging mechanism might be open to fraud. Some unit holders might rig high prices and so increase numbers of units owned, and then spend or sell them before any market correction. Managers may be wiser to judge before reacting. But the automatic model shows how quick and inexpensive pegging can be. Diversified funds should be easier to peg than single issues because their price fluctuations tend to be smoothed by averaging. Other things equal, dollar-pegged units should be preferred as money to dollar-pegged shares for easier pegging and greater stability in yield.

A CENTRAL FUND SCENARIO

Many mutual funds today are checkable. Unit holders receive checkbooks much as depositors do. Checks are drawn on the fund's bank deposit, not the unit holder's, and the fund then sells enough of the holder's units to make itself whole. Here units are readily convertible into bank money at whatever current prices for units may be. They do not *back* money and so do nothing to relieve problems of controlling its supply. But this checkability should help disarm an argument that the world is psychologically unready for fund money.

In my scenario, dollar-pegged units are themselves money. When the seller cashes the buyer's mutual fund check, dollar-pegged units are transferred from the buyer's unit holding account to the seller's. Bank money plays no part.

There might be one or more central funds corresponding to the central bank of today. Membership in a central fund would be voluntary. Member funds might collectively own most of their units. Central funds might be debt-neutral index funds for greater strength and balance and would serve for check clearing as central banks do now. Meanwhile member banks may cater to different investment philosophies. Some may favor leveraged equities for high yield, and some may favor short-term notes for stability. A buyer's check for a hundred dollars may be drawn on a high-yield fund, say, while a seller's fund may maximize stability. Say both funds have holdings in a central fund's units. A hundred dollars worth of these is transferred from the former fund's holding to the latter's as the buyer's check clears, much as in the Federal Reserve Bank today.

Central funds might also issue "bearer units" analogous to present-day currency. These could be convertible at bearer's option into units of any member fund. Until converted they might be yieldless, as bank currency is. Ways to make them fully yielding also exist, but need not be discussed here. Since some fund money would be owned for spending and some for yield, subsidized check-processing costs would no longer be practical. Full costs would have to be calculated and charged.

Mixed Money

As mentioned, bank money is layered and imperfectly fungible. Currency differs from deposits in yield and stability, and these from one another. So it may prove with mutual fund money. Not all funds will be debt neutral. There will be leveraged ones for the adventurous, and debt funds for the risk averse. All these funds may have dollar-pegged units that can serve as money. Although I showed that these can be made to hold equal in market value indefinitely, they will differ in yield and volatility. To repeat, perfectly fungible money is no more a part of my scenario than it is of the world today.

The Outlook for Banks

What will happen to banks when they no longer monopolize the creation and storage of money? It seems to me that short-term debt mutual funds of high security will be able to outcompete them in both size and steadiness of yield to depositors. Risk-averse investors seem to belong elsewhere than in the business of value-uncertain retail lending even if they hold senior interests there. But if banks cannot keep depositors, perhaps they can replace them with owners. Banks can evolve into mutual banks. In my terms these would amount to debt mutual funds specializing in community loans. Debt to depositors would disappear, and banks at one step would shed their historic instability. Shares or units in them could be dollar-pegged so that banks could continue to be an important source of money.

Transition

Dollar-pegging is virtually costless, as I argued, and should bring new demand for units as money. Pegged units would then hold a market advantage over unpegged ones. This would give funds an incentive to peg. Suppose some do. Fund money then grows gradually at the expense of bank money because of its advantage in yield. Central bank managers gradually lessen the supply of bank money to keep its value up. The two kinds of money coexist while fund money develops its institutions and gains recognition.

When bank money shrinks in supply or disappears, fund money must peg itself to something else. In effect, the new target will be the dollar of recent memory, just as it is for central bank managers now. The difference is that stable bank money must hold a steady ratio to current output, while stable fund money holds a steady ratio to fund value. Fund value can grow to any size, limited by world wealth, and fund money can be stable in very large supply.

The Double Target

My argument on double criticality questioned whether an ideal supply of bank money exists. Assuming it does, I said that economists disagree on ways of spotting monetary targets and hitting them. In a world of fund money these issues might be treated as follows.

What I said about the efficiency point implies that people would hold more bank money if it bore no holding costs. That's because this point balances holding costs and transaction costs. If the former disappeared, more money could save more of the latter. Unit money has no holding cost, no efficiency point, and no stability point. Its ideal supply is very large so long as number of units and aggregate fund value move in step. Since both these variables should be easy to track, it seems technically easy to hit monetary targets fast and accurately. And so long as the target continues to be the bank dollar, there should be no mystery in finding the number of units that will keep values there.

This leaves two questions. How does one translate technical possibility into administrative practice, and how does one spot targets after the bank dollar recedes?

As for the first question, in my scenario member funds would probably have to accept central fund guidelines for stock splits and reverse splits as a condition of membership. Otherwise convertibility into central fund units might not make sense. Member funds would have to dollar-peg individually, but under close oversight and control of central funds. If there was more than one central fund, any two would pretty clearly have to agree on unit number for funds that were members of both. This agreement might work through a joint committee of rotating chairmanship or through an agreed division of responsibility.

As regards the second question, what happens when the target becomes a remembered dollar rather than an actually spendable one? Then central funds, like today's central banks, will be on their own. But they will have an advantage to start with. They will have two equivalent targets to spot. They can track purchasing power just as monetary authorities do today. But they can also track asset value of their own debt-neutral diversified portfolios. They might do so by estimating current real growth rates of firms represented, much as monetarists do today. Then they can adjust number of units to match. The targets are equivalent because only market-recognized inherent value determines purchasing power of debt-neutral fund money.

Risk Immunity

As noted, central fund managers will aim to hold debt-neutral units constant in asset value and implicitly in purchasing power. Meanwhile markets will arbitrage between these units and debt-fund units. So long as units of both kinds are interchangeable, debt units are effectively backed by debt-neutral ones and so by hard assets. Debt today is more immune from business risks and equity from money instability risks. Debt-fund units in my scenario can combine these immunities.

The Tilted Playing Field

Many people, including myself, believe that modern economies are overleveraged. The consequences include instability of equity interests, and therefore suboptimal business foresight. I implied that a shift from junior debt to equity might well mean improvement in both profit and steadiness. Like others, I found our main debt-inducing laws to be deposit insurance subsidies, bank regulation restricting equity investment, the double tax, and home mortgage deductibility. I urged that all should be repealed or neutralized with the proviso that the first two should disappear together or not at all.

Banks and others have suffered alike from overleverage. Stock banks are the most leveraged firms yet known, and they are primarily debt intermediaries. Bank money is debt collateralized by debt. I do maintain that a considerable change in bank structure and in the genesis of money must be part of any normalization of leverage.

Fund money is plausible even on the tilted playing field. Deleveraging should make it stabler and should add urgency to its development if bank money should prove unable to compete on a level field.

International Fund Money

A fund might pool securities of many countries, and thus yield returns in many currencies. Units might be pegged to any one of them or to some other standard. An international fund would be debt neutral if debt instruments from each country offset debt load in equities from that country.

Meanwhile some ex-communist countries may lack stable currencies and settled economic institutions. Some of these are auctioning off shares in ex-state companies to their citizens and others. These shares have greatest value when the companies are well run and profitable. They are most likely to be so if international businesses can be attracted to operate or buy them and to invest in them. Attracting those businesses will mean first establishing clear property rights and protecting market freedom.

Citizens might sell shares in ex-state companies and buy units in international debt-neutral mutual funds. If suitably pegged, these units can serve as stable and profitable money. Ex-communist countries need not repeat our failed experiments. Bank money has brought us three centuries of crisis and one of inflation. Others may as well start off on the right foot.

Mutual funds today are few and small outside the United States, and debt-neutral ones exist nowhere. But funds can grow quickly. My scenario visualizes a centrol role for them in a postinflationary world, both here and abroad.

ROBERT E. LITAN

Fertile Money and Banks in Russia: A Comment

Gordon Getty has written a fascinating and provocative paper about the role of money. As it turns out, however, the ideas advanced in his paper are more relevant to the United States than to Russia. I will explain why as I proceed.

THE PROBLEM WITH BANKS

It is perhaps useful to begin by summarizing what I understand to be Getty's main arguments. In the process, I use some literary license to translate Getty's claims into the economic language I find more familiar.

Getty starts by noting that money is whatever individuals and firms accept as a medium of exchange. In modern economies, both currency issued by the state (or its central bank) and deposits at banks or other depository institutions have fit this definition. In practice, however, deposits are much more important. For example, at the end of 1992 in the United States there was $292 billion in currency outstanding as against $726 billion held in checking accounts in commercial banks and savings and loans and nearly $2.5 trillion in money market funds, money market accounts at banks, and savings and small-time deposits held in banks and thrifts.

There is a problem with bank deposits, however. As banks and other depository institutions have evolved, they have invested the potentially liquid deposits they have collected—that is, funds which can be with-

This paper is a revised version of oral comments I provided at the January, 1993, conference. Since attending that conference, I have become involved in a Treasury-financed program that provides technical assistance to bankers in Russia and the Ukraine.

drawn promptly at any time by account holders—primarily in illiquid loans, which usually cannot be turned into "money" as quickly. In addition, depository institutions have been allowed to become highly leveraged; that is, the ratio of deposit liabilities to shareholder's capital, about 15 or 20 to 1, is much higher than the ratio of liabilities to capital in other types of enterprise (financial or nonfinancial). In combination, high leverage and the coupling of bank deposits with illiquid loans render bank deposit money potentially highly unstable. When one bank fails, depositors at other banks can get nervous and withdraw their funds, triggering a chain reaction of bank failures, an "implosion" of the money supply, and thus a severe contraction of economic activity.

Getty does not discuss this extensively in his paper, but most industrialized countries have adopted deposit insurance to forestall this nightmare scenario. And deposit insurance, coupled with implicit government guarantees of nominally uninsured deposits at large banks, has worked: to my knowledge, there have been no serious deposit runs in any advanced country since the Depression despite many failures of individual banks.

But government guarantees of bank deposits have a price, which economists have labeled the moral hazard problem: the presence of insurance relaxes the incentives of banks to avoid excessive risks. During the 1980s and early 1990s the United States paid more than $200 billion in bank and thrift failure costs to learn this fundamental lesson. Recently, Japan, Sweden, and Norway—all of which have major problems in their banking sectors—have also learned that their banks are not immune to moral hazard.

Bank money also has another problem, according to Getty. Money is costly to hold because, although it may bear interest, in the case of bank deposits it earns less than alternative, less liquid, assets. At the same time, money enables its holders to enter into transactions. Getty suggests that individuals and firms will thus want to hold "just that amount of money at which the marginal transaction advantage and the marginal holding cost are expected to cancel out." This amount of money, in turn, will support at any given price level a certain volume of transactions or output. Push the supply of money higher than the willingness of individuals to hold it, and an economy will get inflation as "too much money chases too few goods."

A key problem, according to Getty, is that government planners— or central bankers—cannot know if the relationship between money and output, or the velocity of money, is stable. As a result, even if the money supply could be perfectly controlled (which is not the case, since banks influence bank deposit creation by how willing they are to extend loans), the central bank does not know whether velocity will go up or down, and thus cannot know whether a given monetary expansion will increase output or prices or do nothing at all.

THE GETTY SOLUTION: FERTILE MONEY

Getty has a simple solution to the two problems with bank money—its potential instability and its uncertain relation to economic activity: allow shares in mutual funds to serve as money. In Getty's world, shareholders of the Fidelity, T. Rowe Price, or Vanguard funds would be able to go to the grocery store and use the shares in these funds to pay for food without first converting the shares to cash and then using the cash to buy goods. Each of the shares would be denominated in dollar units, presumably just like dollar bills, although the number of such units held by any shareholder would vary daily in accordance with changes in the prices of the underlying securities in which the funds were invested. A central clearinghouse, presumably a private version of the Federal Reserve Bank, would clear the movements of mutual fund shares between buyers and sellers. Mutual fund money would be "fertile," in Getty's sense of the term, because it would yield higher rates of return than current bank deposits.

Getty argues that such a system would solve his two problems with bank money. Mutual funds, or fertile money, would not be subject to "runs," since mutual fund shares and the assets that back them are liquid. If investors want to get out of their mutual funds, they risk a decline in the value of their shares. But theoretically no mutual fund shareholder can face the risk of losing all of his or her funds, as would happen to the unlucky uninsured bank depositor who asks for his or her money back only to find out that the depositors who were there first drained the bank of its assets.

Getty does not really explain how fertile money would lead to greater economic stability, and I must confess that I cannot do any better.

It is true that the holding costs of fertile money would be lower than bank money, because by definition fertile money supplies a competitive rate of return. Indeed, if Getty is right that because of its higher returns his fertile money would drive out bank money, then, except for currency, the money supply would become fully privatized. The reason is that the supply of mutual fund shares depends solely on the available supply of underlying securities, whose issuance is decided by private firms. Similarly, the demand for mutual fund shares depends solely on private behavior—specifically, whether individuals, firms, and other private agents want to hold shares in a fund rather than in the underlying securities or deposits in banks. In such a world, the central bank can still influence economic activity through its purchases and sales of government securities, which in turn influence the level of short-term interest rates. But the quantity of "money" would essentially be outside the central bank's control.

Although such a situation may be desirable to those who don't trust the Fed's ability to reduce economic volatility (a view I personally don't share), I fail to see how totally privatized money provides any greater degree of macroeconomic stability. That is, I see no reason for believing that the velocity of fertile money—that is, its relation to output—would be any more stable than the velocity of currency and bank money. Moreover, why would the market produce any more stable a growth path of fertile money than the Fed now produces in bank money? The public's appetite for mutual fund shares, as opposed to ownership in individual stocks, waxes and wanes. So does the growth of the raw material for mutual funds—the underlying stocks and bonds—issued by private companies.

Getty closes his paper by claiming the advantages of a variation of fertile money for ex-communist countries like Russia. He observes that such countries may (and in the case of Russia certainly do) lack stable currencies. Why not permit them to buy units in international mutual funds, whose shares could serve as money? In effect, Getty urges that such countries effectively abandon their current currencies and use foreign money instead. Such a solution, in his view, would bring order to the current chaotic process of money creation in those countries and thus presumably bring a halt to inflation.

A CRITIQUE

If Getty's proposal sounds revolutionary, it isn't, at least for the United States. The fact is that fertile money already is essentially here, although in not as plentiful supply as Getty would want. The current fertile money consists of mutual funds with check-writing privileges, which provide the functional equivalent of "moneyness" to those funds. To be sure, checks drawn on mutual funds must be cleared thorugh a bank first, but that is a technical detail. The fundamental fact is that as long as customers can use their mutual shares as a means of payment, those shares indeed are fertile in Getty's sense of the term.

The only important practical difference between the fertile money that Getty advocates and the fertile money that now exists is the size of the transactions for which they would be used. Under the current framework, mutual funds usually require each check to exceed some minimum threshhold (typically $250 or $500). In Getty's world, mutual fund money could be used with much fewer restrictions, perhaps as freely as ordinary bank checks now.

Accordingly, if it were effective, Getty's proposal would only accelerate the replacement of bank deposits with mutual fund shares, a process that has been going on now for at least the last two decades. In the long run, that is a desirable outcome, since it would further reduce the share of financial assets that are backed by federal guarantees. That isn't the main reason Getty advances for his proposal, but it is the only one I find persuasive.

Getty also believes fertile money would provide advantages to individuals as well, for it would enable them to earn higher returns on funds they normally would use for transactions purposes. But if that is true, why don't mutual funds that allow check writing now under limited circumstances relax those restrictions and give individuals freer access to their funds? The obvious answer is that to do so would be expensive, both by adding to processing cost and by creating more uncertainty about the timing of redemptions. In theory, the funds could charge fees to cover the additional costs, but the level at which such charges would be set would probably discourage shareholders from using the service. Or at least that appears to be the judgment the market has implicitly rendered, since no funds now offer unlimited checking.

In short, there doesn't seem to be a demand for Getty's fertile money. Getty may respond that there would be if someone could come along and provide a clearing service cheaper than the check- or wire-clearing services now offered by the Fed. Maybe so. But Getty in this paper hasn't demonstrated that this is possible with current technology.

FERTILE MONEY AND RUSSIA

Regardless of the merits of the fertile money concept for the United States, the relevant question for this conference is whether the idea has any applicability to Russia and other ex-communist countries.

If by fertile money one means mutual fund shares backed by *domestic* securities, the answer is clear: the idea simply isn't practical and wouldn't be for some time to come. The reason is that securities markets in ex-communist countries are in their infancy and there simply isn't sufficient raw material in the form of securities underlying mutual fund shares to serve as a meaningful supply of money. Moreover, the securities markets in these countries are still relativley illiquid, so that in a fundamental sense the balance sheets of mutual funds look very much like banks: liquid shares backed by illiquid investments. In such an environment, the mutual funds are subject to the same kind of "run" problem to which banks are subject. The first to withdraw can get all their funds back; latecomers may get left with the crumbs. Knowing that, all of the holders of the shares have incentives to redeem them at once at the first sign that the funds may not have sufficient liquid assets on hand to meet a significant increase in the demand for redemptions.

What about Getty's suggestion that citizens of the ex-communist countries be entitled to use fertile money backed by foreign currency— denominated securities, or instruments issued in markets where liquidity is not a problem? The aspect of the proposal that relies on foreign currencies is not new. So-called hard currencies, such as the dollar and the deutsche mark, are already used as currency in these countries, although as a matter of practice rather than explicit law. Getty's proposal would formalize the use of foreign currency in domestic transactions, but with the additional wrinkle that mutual fund shares denominated in foreign currency would qualify as well.

As mentioned, this plan essentially suggests that the ex-communist countries abandon their domestic currencies; or alternatively that they adopt "currency boards," which peg the volume of domestic currency to foreign currency reserves. From what little I know about these countries, such proposals are politically unrealistic, since each government seems devoted to having its own money supply and controlling it. In addition, though the use of foreign currencies would stop inflation, it also would represent the harshest form of shock therapy, effectively ending all the subsidies to firms now implicitly provided through a liberal monetary policy.

This is not the place to debate the merits of shock therapy. But if such a policy is desirable, it can be accomplished more readily and simply either by halting domestic currency creation or by adopting the currency bond concept.

GENNADY M. DANILENKO

International Law and the Future of Rechtsstaat *in* Russia

The revolutionary changes in eastern Europe and Russia have opened unique opportunities for the rule of law at the international level. The transformation of almost all the totalitarian societies of the former communist bloc into new democracies has brought about a new international community. Indeed, the decline of East-West rivalry may have inaugurated a new era for the development of international law and its implementation. Rule making at the European–North American regional level, in particular within the Helsinki process, has been an unprecedented success. The adoption of the Copenhagen final document and the Paris Charter not only strengthens long-standing norms protecting human rights but also for the first time defines the essential parameters of a democratic and law-based state capable of guaranteeing these rights.[1] International regulation thus acquires a new quality and reaches areas that until recently were exclusively within the domestic jurisdiction of states.

Of great interest in this connection is the changing attitude of Russia to international law, specifically to the status of international law in its domestic law. As a nation committed to the building of a state based on law, Russia has made significant progress toward providing legal guarantees for internationally protected human rights in its domestic legal system. The potential impact of this development on a new world order based on the rule of law is far more important than votes and policy statements made at different international forums. The incorporation of international standards is also of crucial importance for the advancement of a state based on the rule of law in Russia.

This paper first addresses the changes in the Russian attitude toward international law in its domestic legal setting. I describe, against the background of the previous Soviet experience, the recent efforts to incorporate international law. An analysis of the practice of the newly established Constitutional Court follows. The principal provisions of the Draft Constitution concerning the relationship between international and Russian domestic law is then reviewed. Finally, I evaluate the significance of these developments for a law-based state in Russia.

SOVIET LEGAL SYSTEM AND INTERNATIONAL LAW

The former Soviet Union never regarded international law, especially human rights law, as something that might be invoked by its domestic courts. The 1977 Constitution did not allow direct operation of international law within the domestic setting.[2] Although the Constitution proclaimed that the relations of the USSR with other states shall be built on the basis of the principle of "fulfillment in good faith of obligations arising from the generally recognized principles and rules of international law, and from international treaties signed by the USSR," this broad clause was never interpreted as a general incorporation of international norms into Soviet domestic law.[3] Though application of international norms was envisaged in some exceptional cases of treaty law, as a matter of general constitutional principle the Soviet legal order remained closed to international legal norms.

The Soviet legal system was protected from any direct penetration of international law by the concept that recognizes international law and municipal law as two completely separate legal systems. As a result of this dualist approach, in order to be applicable internally, international obligations have to be transformed into separate statutes or administrative regulations. The Soviet Union was thus able to sign many international treaties, including treaties on human rights, and still abstain from implementing all or some of their provisions.

The absence of a constitutional rule providing for a direct incorporation of international law into Soviet domestic law was not accidental. This state of affairs reflected the long-standing isolationist tendency in Soviet society in general and in the Soviet legal system in particular. In the early years of the Soviet state, the distrust toward international law was explained by the prevailing ideology aimed at a complete destruction of the world order.

The Soviet Union also rejected a number of principles of the then existing international law, in particular those relating to expropriations of foreign property.

The movement toward reform of the preexisting "closed" legal system began only with the advent of *perestroika*. The leaders of the Soviet Union had realized that at the new stage of technological evolution the country had no prospects for further economic and social development. A modern society based on the idea of the rule of law would have to be built up in the USSR. An important element of the overall reform was the recognition that the country would have to ensure that internationally accepted norms were observed.

Many international commitments in the area of human rights assumed by the USSR in previous years suddenly became a source for political reform. The focus on international law was motivated by several political-legal considerations. First, there was a broad consensus among policymakers and citizens that internal laws of the Soviet Union lagged behind legal standards at the international level. Second, there was more trust in international institutions than in national authorities, which had lost much of their legitimacy. Third, international standards enjoyed a high degree of legitimacy resulting from their prior (even if only oral) acceptance by the Soviet Union and their general acceptance by "the civilized nations." The legitimacy of international human rights standards was also based on the perception that they expressed universal human values.

Although reformers pressed for a comprehensive legal reform of Soviet law, such a reform was clearly not easy. Many policymakers and lawyers argued that the gradual transformation of international standards into new legislative acts should be accompanied by a radical constitutional reform. Such a reform would require the Soviet Union to accept a general constitutional principle proclaiming international law as part of the law of the land. Although the former USSR never managed to adopt such a principle, the 1989 Law on Constitutional Supervision introduced major changes into the preexisting legal situation.[4] For the first time in Soviet history, a law provided a mechanism for the direct incorporation of various international rules into the Soviet domestic legal system. It gave to the Committee of Constitutional Supervision the power to review domestic laws by reference to international obligations of the USSR. By introducing the concept of direct relevance of international law to the internal legal process, the country took a giant step away from its previous isolationist stand.

During its short period of work, the Committee of Constitutional Supervision relied on international law in more than half its decisions.

I will mention only a few. Already in its first decision, which declared unconstitutional a number of legislative acts that excluded certain labor disputes from the jurisdiction of the courts,[5] the committee relied on articles 7 and 8 of the United Nations Universal Declaration of Human Rights and article 2, paragraph 3, of the UN Covenant of Civil and Political Rights. Another decision of the committee challenged the existing norms of criminal law and procedure that violated the presumption of innocence.[6] The last decision of the committee, handed down just before the collapse of the Soviet Union, concerned the constitutionality of the infamous regulations requiring residence permits. In declaring all regulations requiring residence permits unconstitutional, the committee gave special weight to such international acts as the Universal Declaration of Human Rights and the Covenant on Civil and Political Rights.[7]

THE CHANGING STATUS OF INTERNATIONAL LAW IN RUSSIA'S DOMESTIC LAW

The newly independent Russia inherited from its Soviet past a constitution that, like all other Soviet constitutions, did not envisage direct application of international law by domestic courts. The "opening" of the Russian domestic legal system to international law become one of the most important elements of the ongoing constitutional reform.

At this stage, constitutional reforms in Russia are implemented within two different law-making procedures. The first procedure involves a step-by-step reform of the existing 1977 Constitution. During the last several years the Russian Congress of People's Deputies, which has an exclusive jurisdiction over constitutional changes, has enacted a number of amendments that have changed almost 75 percent of the clauses of the old text. First, while the existing text still contains many obsolete provisions and contradictions,[8] the reformers were able to introduce extensive innovations in key sections dealing with the form of government, human rights, federal structure, and the judicial system. Second, the congress decided to draft an entirely new constitution. It established a Constitutional Commission, which has submitted a draft of the new Constitution.[9] In April 1992 the congress approved the draft by adopting a resolution that endorsed "the basic provisions" of the future Constitution.[10] In December 1992 the congress approved the proposal to hold a referendum on "the fundamental provisions of the new Constitution."[11] It was anticipated that after the referendum the new Constitution, which incorporates all the earlier patchwork revisions, would be submitted to the congress for final approval. The schedule has been overtaken by events, and at this time it is difficult to predict when the new Constitution will be submitted to popular vote and how many further changes will be made.

In view of the past massive violations of human rights in Russia, the drafters of new constitutional provisions place special emphasis on domestic implementation of international human rights standards. In November 1991 the congress adopted the Declaration of the Rights and Freedoms of Man and Citizen.[12] An important element of the declaration is a general clause that incorporates international norms for human rights into the Russian domestic law. Article 1 of the declaration provides that "the generally recognized international norms concerning human rights have priority over laws of the Russian Federation and directly create rights and obligations for the citizens of the Russian Federation." In April 1992 the declaration, including article 1, became part of the existing 1977 Constitution.

These normative innovations have been accompanied by a general reform of the judicial system. An important development is the adoption of the idea of constitutional control as a constituent element of democracy. In 1991 the parliament enacted the Law on the Constitutional Court—the first court in Russian history to be given a competence to decide constitutional issues.[13] Under the law, the Constitutional Court is granted broad powers to review the constitutionality of statutory legislation and other normative acts. The court also has the power to control the constitutionality of decisions and of the "law-applying practice" of all ordinary courts, other state organs, and officials as regards their consistency with the constitutional provisions for human rights. Constitutional review of a "law-applying" practice violating human rights may come to the court through an indidividual constitutional complaint.[14] Any private person may file individual complaints challenging the constitutionality of a law-applying practice" violating "fundamental rights and lawful interests" protected by the Constitution—a dramatic breakthrough for human rights in Russia.

The newly established Constitutional Court has already decided many important cases. The record of the court indicates that it is becoming an important institution promoting the idea of direct application of international law and, of course, establishing the concept of judicial review.

The first case in which the Constitutional Court relied on international law originated within the "individual complaint procedure." The *Labor Code Case* concerned the controversial practice of using a simplified procedure for annulling labor contracts with persons who have reached pension age.[15] The court held that such simplified procedures for annulling labor contracts violated the principle of nondiscrimination in the Constitution. The court also gave an innovative broad interpretation of the general provision of the Constitution which proclaims that "foreign political activities of the Russian Federation shall be based on the recognition and respect" of the principle of "fulfillment in good faith of obligations and other generally recognized principles and rules of international law."[16] The court held that in the Russian domestic context all courts must "assess the applicable law from the point of view of its conformity with the principles and rules of international law."[17] Furthermore, the court noted that the Declaration of the Rights and Freedoms of Man and Citizen ensures that the generally recognized international norms for human rights should be given priority over laws of the Russian Federation and that such norms directly create rights and obligations for the citizens of the Russian Federation.[18]

In another case involving labor relations, the court found that certain procedural norms and practices restricting the right of plaintiffs in labor disputes to appeal against the decisions of lower courts violate the right to an effective remedy by a court of law. In support of its decision, which declared the relevant restrictions unconstitutional, the court cited the Universal Declaration of Human Rights, the Covenant on Civil and Political Rights, and the Covenant on Economic, Social and Cultural Rights.[19]

The Constitutional Court also relied on international law in the *Tatarstan Case*.[20] The controversy involved an attempt by Tatarstan, a constituent republic of the Russian Federation, to break away from Russia.[21] At issue were the unilateral steps undertaken by Tatarstan to proclaim itself an independent state. Furthermore, the court had to determine the constitutionality of the proposed referendum on independence. Although the court declared the unilateral secessionist steps unconstitutional on the basis of the existing Constitution, it also drew support from international law. According to the court, the principle of self-determination does not necessarily provide a legal ground for separatism: it may be realized in different forms, such as the establishment of a sovereign and independent state, the free association or integration with an independent state, or the emergence into any other political status. The court found that the observance of other principles of international law, in particular the principle of the territorial integrity of states, must also be observed. The court held that the unilateral succession of Tatarstan from the Russian Federation would violate the principle of the territorial integrity of Russia and legal principles protecting the rights of individuals and peoples. The proposed referendum on independence was thus declared to be unconstitutional.

These cases show that although the existing Russian Constitution still lacks a general provision expressly incorporating international law, by its innovative interpretation of certain broad constitutional principles the Constitutional Court has provided a firm legal ground for the direct application of international norms by national tribunals. The *Labor Code Case* and the *Tatarstan Case* demonstrate that not only norms relating to human rights but also other pertinent international norms may be involved nationally. While lower courts, which have no experience in applying international law, are still cautious about turning to its principles, the ground-breaking decisions of the Constitutional Court are paving the way for a broader application of international legal norms. Although other provisions have changed greatly in light of the shifting political controversies, the international issues have remained a part of each new version of the much amended Draft Constitution.

INTERNATIONAL LAW IN THE DRAFT CONSTITUTION

The issue of ensuring compliance with international obligations figures prominently in current constitutional debate. The Draft Constitution, indeed, contains an unprecedented number of references to international law. Broadly speaking, the draft seeks to confirm the current trend toward giving a prominent place to international legal standards in the domestic legal setting. A principal aim of the draft is further clarification of the domestic constitutional status of international law.

The draft also broadens the powers of the Constitutional Court in the application of international law.

The general philosophy of the draft constitution on international matters is reflected in a number of provisions which confirm that Russia considers itself part of the "world community."[22] As a state committed to the rule of law,[23] Russia intends to respect "the generally recognized principles and norms of international law" and "international treaties."[24] The draft emphasizes that the Russian Federation ensures human rights according to "the generally recognized principles and norms of international law."[25] Besides these general provisions, the draft contains a special article on the status of international law in Russian domestic law. Article 3 states:

> The generally recognized principles and norms of international law and international treaties ratified by the Russian Federation constitute part of its law. If a ratified international treaty of the Russian Federation establishes other rules than those which are contained in laws, the rules of this international treaty shall be applied.

This extremely important constitutional norm has several basic features:

First, draft article 3 clearly states that international law becomes part of Russian law. As a result, individuals may invoke international law, as part of the law of the land, before all national tribunals.

Second, draft article 3 incorporates into the Russian law not only treaty law but also "the generally recognized principles and norms of international law." This obviously includes general customary law.

Third, draft article 3 embraces the principles and norms binding on Russia at this juncture and also principles and norms that Russia might accept in the future. This is an important step because Russia is planning to join the Council of Europe. Since the ideas of democracy, of the rule of law, and of human rights pervade the whole statute of the Council of Europe, joining will strengthen and accelerate the domestic evolution toward democracy and legal reform.

Fourth, draft article 3 allows law-enforcement agencies to take note of the interpretation of international treaties by competent international bodies, such as the International Court of Justice.

Fifth, draft article 3 establishes a higher normative status for treaty rules than for contrary domestic laws. This means that legal regulations in force within Russia shall not apply if this application is incompatible with treaty provisions.

The Draft Constitution envisages the Constitutional Court as the principal domestic forum for resolving constitutional disputes. Because the Draft Constitution declares international law part of Russian law, the court will be able to reaffirm its prior practice of relying on international law when resolving constitutional disputes. The same constitutional provision will also provide a firmer basis for the application of international law by all other state agencies. It may therefore be assumed that the adoption of a new constitution, whatever its broad provisions on executive-legislative relations, will consolidate gains achieved in the areas of international law and adoption of human rights standards.

INTERNATIONAL LAW AND
ITS SIGNIFICANCE FOR RUSSIA

The current constitutional debate suggests that Russia has embraced the idea of direct application in national tribunals of international law as part of a general policy aimed at advancing the rule of law. The idea of rule of law as a control over official action will lead to greater compliance with international law. In a democracy based on the rule of law it is extremely difficult to conceal governmental actions that violate internationally accepted standards. The rule of law in Russia thus provides additional guarantees that the country will not violate its international obligations. Of particular importance is the extension of international law down to individual men and women. The emergence of Russian domestic courts as organs capable of applying international law will strengthen the enforcement machinery of the international legal system, which continues to rely on the domestic structures of individual states.

The opening of the Russian legal system provides external guarantees for the continued democratization of Russia. The direct relevance of international law for the internal legal process will consolidate the domestic rule of law and strengthen the level of protection of human rights. Although the existing Constitution contains an elaborate catalogue of human rights, many subconstitutional norms contained in ordinary legislation and administrative regulations do not conform to international standards. International law reinforces the legitimacy of the constitutional and other legal norms adopted in recent years. In situations where Russian statutory laws fall below international standards, international law may become an important direct source of law. International standards may thus be used as a legitimate legal ground for abolishing outdated domestic norms. This function of international law is important in that the comprehensive reform of Russian laws now under way is likely to take many years. In the meantime, international law will provide certain basic elements for human rights and democracy and may exert a stabilizing influence on Russia as it lives through a period of revolutionary change and unprecedented legal development.

NOTES

1. "Conference on Security and Co-operation in Europe: Document of the Copenhagen Meeting of the Conference on the Human Dimension," reprinted in *International Legal Materials*, vol. 29 (1990); and "Charter of Paris for a New Europe," reprinted in ibid., vol. 30 (1991).

2. See "Konstitutsia (Osnovnoi zakon) Soiuza Sovetskikh Sotsialisticheskikh Respublik" [Constitution (fundamental law) of the Union of Soviet Socialist Republics], *Svod zakonov SSSR*, vol. 1 (Code of laws of the USSR). For an English translation of the 1977 Constitution, see Albert P. Blaustein and Gisbert H. Flanz, eds., *Constitutions of the Countries of the World* (Dobbs Ferry, N.Y.: Oceana Publications, 1991).

3. For details, see G. M. Danilenko, "Soviet Constitutional Reforms and International Human Rights Standards," *Collected Courses of the Academy of European Law*, vol. 1, no. 2 (Boston: Dordrecht, 1992), pp. 239–40.

4. "Zakon SSSR O konstitutsionnom nadzore v SSSR" (Law of the USSR on constitutional supervision in the USSR), *Vedomosty Siezda narodnykh deputatov SSSR i Verkhovnogo Soveta SSSR*, no. 29, item 572 (1989) (Official gazette of the Congress of People's Deputies and Supreme Soviet of the USSR (hereafter *Vedomosty SSSR*); as amended in 1990, see *Vedomosty SSSR*, no. 12, item 189, para. 14 (1990).

5. *Vedomosty SSSR*, no. 27, item 524 (1990).

6. *Vedomosty SSSR*, no. 39, item 775 (1990).

7. *Rossiiskaya Gazeta*, October 15, 1992, p. 1.

8. Thus, although article 3 of the 1977 Constitution proclaims the principle of the separation of powers, a number of other provisions, which reflect traditional Soviet concepts, contradict it. For example, article 2 asserts the tradi-

tional Soviet dogma by declaring that the people exercise their state power only "through Soviets of people's deputies." Article 104 reflects the traditional theory that all power has to be concentrated in the hands of the Supreme Soviet by stating that the Congress of People's Deputies may debate and "decide any question" falling within the jurisdiction of the Russian Federation.

9. "Proekt Konstitutsii Rossiiskoi Federatsii" (Draft Constitution of the Russian Federation) (1992) (hereafter Draft Constitution).

10. "O proekte Konstitutsii Rosiiskoi Federatsii" (On the Draft Constitution of the Russian Federation), *Vedomosty RF*, no. 18, item 979 (1992).

11. *Rossiiskaya Gazeta*, December 15, 1992, p. 1.

12. *Vedomosty RF*, no. 52, item 1865 (1992).

13. "Zakon o Konstitutsionnom Sude" (Law on the Constitutional Court), *Vedomosty RF*, no. 19, item 621 (1991).

14. Ibid., articles 1, 2.

15. *Vedomosty RF*, no. 13, item 669 (1992).

16. 1977 Constitution, article 28. See note 2.

17. Ibid.

18. Ibid.

19. *Rossiiskaya Gazeta*, August 4, 1992, p. 5.

20. *Vedomosty RF*, no. 13, item 671 (1992).

21. For details, see G. M. Danilenko, "The New Russian Federalism," *New Europe Law Review*, vol. 1 (forthcoming).

22. Draft Constitution, Preamble, article 11.

23. Ibid., article 1.

24. Ibid., article 11.

25. Ibid., article 2.

E. DONALD ELLIOTT

Environmental Protection and the Development of Free Markets in Russia

How will the new Russia, as it goes about the task of developing free markets and a democratic order, incorporate the idea of environmental protection into its legal culture? If we see environmental protection as a part of what is "social" in the idea of *soziale Marktwirtschaft*, how will this affect the legal order for the development of capitalism?

My topic is to begin to answer such questions by comparing modes of thought about environmental protection in the industrialized countries and their potential relevance for Russia. The topic builds on the notion of differences in legal cultures that Wolfgang Fikentscher and others have spoken about.[1] Also underlying the topic is my belief that international meetings should eschew explicit prescription and focus on a deeper level of philosophic orientation and approaches to common problems. Thus I do not presume to prescribe, or even to suggest, specific institutional approaches to our Russian colleagues. Rather the aim is to present our conceptual models, the way that we look at problems, as raw materials that they may or may not find useful in particular areas.

In that spirit, this paper identifies and analyzes five fundamentally different ways of looking at the problem of environmental protection. These have been developed in part from observing the differences in the fundamental preconceptions at conferences with colleagues from first the Soviet Union and now Russia. The dialogue about legal protection of the environment by Russian colleagues at previous conferences leads me to believe that Russians and Americans view the problem of legal protection of the environment quite differently, reflecting the differences in our prevailing legal cultures.

The five ways of thinking about environmental protection may be divided into three broad groupings or analytical topics. The first concerns prevailing Russian concepts of environmental protection that derive essentially from the legacy of central planning; the second, the two main competing conceptualizations for environmental protection that are dominant in the American legal culture today; the third, an emerging international concept of environmental protection that is different from the reigning American concepts of environmental protection. As regards the third topic, a new consensus is forming in the international community around the concept of "sustainable development."[2] Some scholars have even argued that the philosophy of sustainable development has become part of customary international law.[3] And therefore perhaps, as argued by Danilenko in this volume, such ideas may have become incorporated along with notions of human rights into the Russian legal system.

CURRENT RUSSIAN CONCEPTS: MODE ONE (CONSUMER GOOD) AND MODE TWO (STAGE THEORY)

The two ways of thinking about environmental protection that can be discerned in contemporary Russian thought and practice strike an American lawyer as stemming from a Marxist-Leninist legacy (one also hears them among other members of the former Warsaw Pact). The first characteristic Marxist-Leninist idea might be described as "environment as low-priority consumer good." The basic notion of this concept is that environmental protection competes with the production of television sets, food, and other consumer goods, and takes a relatively low priority in that competition. This way of thinking about environmental protection is not unique to our Russian colleagues. Many conventional Western economists (for example, Michael Boskin, former chairman of the Council of Economic Advisers) at times seem to have thought of environmental protection in the same way—as a consumption good in competion with other goods.

If one thinks of environmental protection as a consumer good in competition with other consumer goods, it will usually have a low priority in circumstances like those now prevailing in Russia. Elsewhere I have described this as the Maslow Value Hierarchy Problem.[4] Some recent research suggests that worldwide pollution levels normally rise until nations achieve a level of gross domestic product (GDP) between $4,000 and $5,000 per capita; they then begin to decline as a wealthier populace demands more protection of the environment.[5]

The second way that Russians think about the environment refects central planning concepts and so might be called the Hegelian, or stage theory of history, approach. This approach is similar to but distinct from the low-priority consumer good idea. The basic notion is that there are discrete stages of development, and to reach any stage one must pass through all the previous stages. In the American and English legal culture, this approach is associated with the philosophy of Herbert Spencer, who drew his models from embryology.[6]

Those who accept this theory of history argue that perhaps at a later stage of institutional development or historical evolution in Russia, it will be time to think about environmental protection. But not now, for there are too many other, more pressing issues.

In the United States, the stage theory of development is not necessarily seen as wrong. The legal historian Morton Horowitz, among others, argues that during the nineteenth century the United States used the system of tort and accident law to subsidize its infant industries.[7] I do not believe Horowitz's theory is correct, but an intellectual pedigree for thinking about the environment in such terms certainly exists.

In effect, the two modes of thought that I have identified so far prevail in discussions with Russian colleagues, but they are not unique to Russia. They also exist as influential minority views within the American legal culture.

CURRENT U.S. CONCEPTS: MODE THREE (MARKET FAILURE) AND MODE FOUR (RELIGIOUS)

The dominant concept of environmental protection in the United States is closely tied to the philosophy of a decentralized market economy. This concept is attractive to those who are interested in evolutionary biology because of a structural parallelism between the decentralized market and the mechanisms of what is sometimes called cybernetic control of populations. The characteristics of populations in evolution resemble the decentralized way in which decisions are made within a market economy.[8]

The underlying theory of the market economy is that the goals of society can best be defined as an aggregation of the preferences of individual consumers functioning in the market. This idea is expressed in pure form by such thinkers as Friedrich Hayek and Milton Friedman.[9] The notion of apprehending the social good through a large number of decentralized decisions made by individuals in a market implies the need to internalize within the decision units the externalities, or social costs, of the decisions. When costs are involuntarily imposed outside of market bargaining, a distortion of market results can occur.

Environmental protection is usually seen in the United States as a particular instance of this need to internalize the external or collateral negative costs, sometimes referred to as a market failure.[10] The essence of the argument is that by the act of polluting, the polluter is able to get all of the benefits in terms of lower operating expenses, but the polluter shares only a portion of the costs of health impairment and other damages. This asymmetry of costs and benefits leads to, in more general terms, a classic case of prisoner's dilemma.[11] That is, we might all be better off if no one polluted, but in the absence of an organization or a structure that allows us to control the actions of others, either through enforcing cooperative bargains or other methods, we may all be led to a suboptimal result. Each person, by maximizing his or her own short-term interest, contributes collectively to a situation that is undesirable from everyone's perspective.

This idea, sometimes called the tragedy of the commons, largely explains why we protect the environment in the American legal system today.[12] The implications of this mode of thought, for the former Soviet Union and for other countries that have recently rejected centralized planning as the method of allocating resources, are most important in terms of the need to create honest hurdle rates for new investments.

The difficulty is this: if one does not internalize the external social costs of pollution, then new projects that pollute can appear to be beneficial from an economic standpoint. If one takes the additional costs caused by pollution damage into account, the project would not result in a net social benefit. To illustrate, consider the case of fission power in the United States. Nuclear power, if one takes into account all the costs of creating the fuel and dealing with the cleanup, may have either an outright negative energy balance or only a small positive benefit.

In a decentralized economy, which makes its resource allocation decisions through the market, mechanisms must be found for explicit social concern for environmental protection, at least for new projects. Hence the need for public policies to promote environmental protection, but, it is hoped, for public policies that are compatible with, and reinforce, decentralized decisionmaking. For new large-scale investment projects in Russia, I would suggest it is critical to try to build in requirements for firms and enterprises to internalize as much as possible the external social costs through taxes, pollution fees, or pricing decisions. Decentralized decisions made in capital markets or markets generally, whether to go ahead with project A or project B, could then be made on the basis most conducive to the long-term social good.

By identifying the economic, or the market failure, argument for pollution controls as the standard intellectual justification for environmental protection, I do not wish to imply that it is noncontroversial. On the contrary, the economic rationale for pollution controls is deeply unsatisfactory to many Americans who believe that protecting the environment is not an economic issue but an ethical matter, perhaps even a religious one.[13] One recent textbook in environmental law contrasts these two competing styles of thinking about the environment in the United States today as "moral outrage" versus "cool analysis."[14] The fundamental basis of the moral outrage mode of thinking is religious—that is, this approach posits appropriate and inappropriate roles and moral duties for human beings in the order of the cosmos.[15] One reason that our domestic dialogue about environmental issues is often so frustrating is that adherents of the analytic and the religious modes of thought are frequently talking past one another. Fikentscher's call for a dialogue on values is relevant here (see his paper in this volume). The way to achieve the truth in a democracy is through dialogue, not through dogma, correct consciousness, or revealed truth.

THE NEW EMERGING INTERNATIONAL CONSENSUS: MODE FIVE (SUSTAINABLE DEVELOPMENT)

Let me turn briefly to the final point, which is the emerging international argument for environmental protection: sustainable development. The logic here is different from that of the four previous approaches. The concept has little to do with the prevailing decentralized market economy concept of pollution control dominant in the United States. The idea behind sustainable development is essentially a moral idea, but not one that turns on revealed truth or any view of the appropriate role of human beings in the cosmos.

The idea of sustainable development was put forth originally and most clearly in the Brundtland Commission Report in 1987.[16] That document sets forth a vision of environmental protection compatible with the market philosophy but not necessarily dependent on it. The sustainable development approach is essentially a moral vision and an intergenerational vision, but one resting on pragmatic arguments about the consequences of environmental neglect.

The central argument is that we as human beings have an obligation to pass on to future generations a world that is as good as the world that we inherited. To those schooled in the American legal culture, this idea will resonate with the thinking of John Locke, who argued in *Two Treatises of Government* that humans may justly appropriate property from nature, but only if "enough and as good" remains for others.

Under this philosophy, any development or economic activity has to be done on a basis that is indefinitely sustainable. In other words, we must design all human activity to be sustainable into the indefinite future, rather than allow the current generation to consume part of the "common patrimony of mankind." The concept of sustainable development is thus based on the idea of intergenerational equity: no living generation is morally entitled to take actions that may harm a future generation, which has an equal entitlement to the earth.

The concept of sustainable development is gaining great acceptance at the international level. For example, it is incorporated into the North American Free Trade Agreement as the standard that will guide future decisions under that treaty between the United States, Canada, and Mexico. These ideas are a shared or common concept among many national legal systems, including Islamic ones. Therefore, as scholars such as Edith Brown Weiss have argued, intergenerational equity has come to be recognized as a principle of customary international law.[17]

The philosophy of sustainable development raises interesting and difficult policy and legal problems. One is the problem of generational horizons. The sustainable development philosophy posits that we have moral obligations to future generations that extend far beyond the biological horizons of our grandchildren or even our great-grandchildren. The problems of environmental protection and sustainable development are increasingly being understood along much longer time scales, time scales of centuries as opposed to short-term issues. But how long a time horizon is appropriate for what category of investment decision?

Let me close with an idea that I hope has relevance for the new Russia. The future well-being of nations depends not only on the economic systems they adopt but also on how they think about the relationship between human beings and the environment. This is illustrated by Yale historian Conrad Totman in an excellent book, *The Green Archipelago*.[18] Totman points out that in the nineteenth century economic conditions in Japan and Haiti were comparable. But in Haiti all the wood on the mountains was cut down and the topsoil was allowed to wash off into the sea. It is now the poorest country in the Western Hemisphere. In Japan, a number of measures were undertaken to regulate the environment (including but not limited to the privatization of property on the mountains, which contributed to conservation because people used their resources more carefully). Japan is, of course, now one of the wealthiest countries in the world. For me, the lesson is clear. Russia has the chance, and the obligation, to fashion a strategy that will create a functioning market system that also protects the future.

NOTES

1. See Wolfgang Fikentscher's contribution in W. Wuellner, ed., *Modes of Thought in Law and Justice: A Preliminary Report on a Study in Legal Anthropology* (Berkeley, Calif.: Center for Hermeneutical Studies in Hellenistic and Modern Culture, 1988). I apply Fikentscher's concept to changes in the style of environmental thinking in the United States in E. Donald Elliott, "Foreword: A New Style of Ecological Thinking in Environmental Law," *Wake Forest Law Review*, vol. 1 (1991).

2. World Commission on Environment and Development, *Our Common Future* (Oxford University Press, 1987). This is known as "The Brundtland Commission Report," named after its chairman, the former Norwegian prime minister, Gro Brundtland.

3. Edith Brown Weiss, *In Fairness to Future Generations: International Law, Common Patrimony, and Intergenerational Equity* (Dobbs Ferry, N.Y.: Transnational Publishers, 1989).

4. Abraham Maslow, a famous American psychologist, posited a hierarchy of human needs, beginning with the need for food and shelter and extending down to various amenities. See, for example, Abraham Maslow, *Motivation and Personality*, 2d ed. (Harper and Row, 1970), pp. 59–60, 97–100. See also E. Donald Elliott, "A Cabin on the Mountain: Reflections on the Distributional Consequences of Environmental Protection Programs," *Kansas Journal of Law and Public Policy*, vol. 1 (1991), p. 5.

5. Gene Grossman and Alan Krueger, "Environmental Impacts of a North American Free Trade Agreement," Wilson School Discussion Paper in Economics 5 (1991), cited in Robert V. Percival and others, *Environmental Regulation: Law, Science and Policy* (Little, Brown, 1992), p. 1192.

6. On evolutionary models drawn from embryology, see E. Donald Elliott, "The Evolutionary Tradition in Jurisprudence," *Columbia Law Review*, vol. 85 (1985), pp. 52–53.

7. Morton Horowitz, *The Transformation of American Law, 1780-1860* (Harvard University Press, 1977), pp. 99–101. For a recent critical challenge to Horowitz's thesis, see Gary Schwartz, "Tort Law and the Economy in Nineteenth Century America: A Reinterpretation," *Yale Law Journal*, vol. 90 (1981), p. 1717.

8. For further elaboration of the similarities between markets and biological evolution, see R. Nelson and S. Winter, *An Evolutionary Theory of Economic Change* (Harvard University Press, 1982).

9. See, in particular, F. A. Hayek, *Law, Legislation and Liberty*, 3 vols. (Chicaco University Press, 1973).

10. For a conventional statement of the paradigm, see Adam Babich, "Understanding the New Era in Environmental Law," *South Carolina Law Review*, vol. 41 (1990) pp. 749–62.

11. See Eric Rasmussen, *Games and Information: An Introduction to Game Theory* (Blackwell, 1989). For the significance of the prisoner's dilemma in biology and political theory, see Roger Masters, *The Nature of Politics* (Yale University Press, 1989), especially chap. 5.

12. Garrett James Hardin, "The Tragedy of the Commons," *Science*, vol. 162 (1968), p. 1243. See also E. Donald Elliott, "Thinking about Conservative Thinkers," *EPA Journal*, Winter 1992.

13. For an early protest that the prevailing economic arguments did not fully capture the real issues, see Rodgers, "Bringing People Back: Toward a Comprehensive Theory of Taking in Natural Resources Law," *Ecology Law Quarterly*, vol. 10 (1982).

14. Percival and others, *Environmental Regulation*, pp. 67–68.

15. See E. Donald Elliott, "Environmental Law at a Crossroad," *North Kentucky Law Review*, vol. 20 (1992), pp. 12–19.

16. World Commission on Environment and Development, *Our Common Future*.

17. See Brown Weiss, *In Fairness to Future Generations*.

18. Conrad Totman, *The Green Archipelago: Forestry in Pre-Industrial Japan* (University of California Press, 1989).

Conference Participants
with their affiliations at the time of the conference

Susan Low Bloch
Professor of Law and Economics
Georgetown University Law School

Robert D. Cooter
Professor of Law and Economics
University of California at Berkeley

Gennady M. Danilenko
Institute of State and Law
Russian Academy of Sciences

John F. Dealy
Distinguished Professor
School of Business
Georgetown University;
Senior Counsel
Shaw, Pittman, Potts, and
  Trowbridge

Gerti Dieker
Assistant to the President
Gruter Institute for Law and
  Behavioral Research

E. Donald Elliott
Julien and Virginia Cornell
  Professor of Environmental
  Law and Litigation
Yale Law School

Wolfgang Fikentscher
Professor of Law
University of Munich

Gordon P. Getty
Consultant

Margaret Gruter
President
Gruter Institute for Law and
  Behavioral Research

Kathryn Hendley
Center for International Security and
  Arms Control
Stanford University

Guy Hormans
Faculté de Droit
Université Catholique
  de Louvain

Viacheslav M. Lebedev
Chief Justice and Chairman of the
  Supreme Court of the Russian
  Federation

Robert E. Litan
Senior Fellow
Economic Studies Program
The Brookings Institution

Lev L. Lubimov
Professor
Institute of World Economy and
  International Relations
Russian Academy of Sciences

Roger D. Masters
Nelson A. Rockefeller Professor of
  Government
Dartmouth College

Michael T. McGuire
Professor of Biobehavioral Science
University of California at
  Los Angeles

Kemer B. Norkin
General Director
The Moscow Mayor's Office

Maxim Sidorov
President
Novick Link Corporation;
Consultant
The Brookings Institution

Bruce L. R. Smith
Senior Staff Member
Center for Public Policy Education
The Brookings Institution

Nina I. Solovianenko
Institute of State and Law
Russian Academy of Sciences

Vasily A. Vlasihin
Senior Research Fellow
Institute of the USA and Canada
Russian Academy of Sciences

Natalia P. Yourina
Deputy Chair of the Board
Ecology and Peace
Moscow

Ivan Zenin
Professor of Law
Moscow State Lomonossov
  University